Techniques and Resources for Guiding Adult Groups

Techniques and Resources for Guiding Adult Groups

Harold D. Minor, editor

ABINGDON PRESS
Nashville
New York

TECHNIQUES AND RESOURCES FOR GUIDING ADULT GROUPS

Library of Congress Cataloging in Publication Data

MINOR, HAROLD D. Techniques and resources for guiding adult groups.
Bibliography: p.
1. Church group work with young adults. I. Title.
BV4446.M5   268'.434   72-2564

ISBN 0-687-41186-6

MANUFACTURED BY THE PARTHENON PRESS AT
NASHVILLE, TENNESSEE, UNITED STATES OF AMERICA

Preface

This book is a companion to *Creative Procedures for Adult Groups,* published in 1968. As in that volume, all the chapters are articles that first appeared in *Adult Leader* (previously *Adult Teacher*).

In selecting these articles, my intention was to avoid duplicating teaching methods that had already appeared in numerous books. Second, it seemed worthwhile to include some suggestions for using resources that are easily available to every teacher. Further, some explanations seemed to be needed of how to use the potential of persons, both group members and guests. Each of these criteria helped to determine which of many excellent pieces would be chosen.

Acknowledgments

During the period when these articles appeared, Mrs. Maxine Stout was nearing the end of a long and significant career in the Division of Curriculum Resources of the United Methodist Board of Education. As assistant editor of *Adult Teacher* (*Adult Leader*), she was the person largely responsible for the original printed version of these articles. I gratefully acknowledge her guidance and assistance through nearly ten years of editorial cooperation.

Also, I take this opportunity to express warm appreciation to Dr. Henry M. Bullock and Dr. Horace R. Weaver. Dr. Bullock made the suggestion for the section in *Adult Teacher* that became "Ways of Teaching-Learning," in which these articles appeared. Dr. Weaver permitted me to continue as editor of this section during a period when I was not editor of the magazine.

Finally, a word of thanks is due the writing friends who prepared the articles, submitted them to the editorial process, and then graciously agreed to the proposal to reprint them in this more permanent form. You and I are indebted to each one whose name appears in the table of contents.

Contents

CONTENTS

Introduction

A New Look at Leadership

Imagine that you have just accepted a position as a group leader in the church. Is it as teacher, class president, work area chairman, age-group coordinator? Will you be responsible for helping a group make decisions or take action? Will you be formulating policies and planning programs and then interpreting them? You may be doing all these. Further, you may need to multiply yourself by recruiting others and supporting them as they carry out some of these actions.

First, you need to decide what your purpose is, and what your attitude toward the job will be. You will ask yourself such questions as these: What kinds of changes need to be made, and how can I help make them? Why is my position needed? What do I hope to achieve? Is this position a challenge or a chore for me? How significant can it become?

What Is Leadership?

Consider the following assumptions about leadership. Do you agree with them?

1. Leadership, for the Christian, is responsible service as part of one's response to the gospel, with laymen and clergymen each fully responsible for ministry.

2. Leadership is exercised in a situation as one interprets it and, for the Christian, with a sense of personal accountability to the total Christian community (the church).

3. Leadership is the exercise of power and influence in interaction with other influences, including one's own personality and history.

4. Leadership is a typical expression of one's whole style of life—aggressive, timid, democratic, and so on.

5. Leadership involves personal aptitudes, as well as skills that can be learned.

6. Leadership expresses a person's own convictions, but should also free and enable others for their own expressions.

7. Leadership is placing one's whole self at the point of need.

How Is Leadership Used?

Next, you need to examine your own ideas of how to lead. Do you think of a good leader mainly as one who makes decisions and then gets others to do what he says? Is a good leader one who is able to guide a group through discussion to a decision by agreement? Or is a good leader one who suggests goals and leaves people free to work on their own?

Each of these styles of leadership (the autocratic, the democratic, and the free-rein) has advantages and disadvantages. Each will be more effective with some persons and less effective with others. Therefore, while your personality may lead you to function generally in one fashion or the other, you will need to vary your approach with specific situations.

Even more important, you should ask yourself, What do I think God wants me to accomplish with my life?

Leaders with long experience in the church know that the most important single factor in successful leadership, especially in teaching, is motivation. If your actions as a leader are guided by a sense of purpose—the conviction that God has something definite for you to do for him— then you will not quickly or easily grow tired of preparing session plans, become angry at indifferent members, or be frustrated by those who disagree with you.

In other words, in your leadership you will try to use the uniqueness of each person (including your own) to the benefit of the group and all the members.

Surely one primary motive of your own in fulfilling your leadership responsibility must be the *pursuit of excellence*. A man known for insistence on excellence is John Gardner, former Secretary of Health, Education, and Welfare. It has been said of Gardner: "Everything he does is focused. He'll say, 'What are the two most important issues? What's the one thing we've got to be doing?' He keeps looking for . . . the most important thing we've got to do in the next six months or so. . . . He connects ideas, people, and resources so that something happens." [1]

The center and focus of the learning transaction is *interaction* between teacher and learner. Your chief task as a teacher is learning how to explore, reflect, communicate,

---

[1] Bernard Asbell, "John Gardner's Own Pursuit of Excellence," *Think*, November-December, 1969, p. 4.

and act. But a second task is to grow in the ability to help learners do the same things and thus foster interaction. For this, a systematic plan is needed.

Your church has responsibility to provide you and other leaders with a program to help you serve with excellence. Such a program will offer assistance in these areas: (1) What are the learners like, and who are they? (2) What does a teacher do? (3) How does a teacher help the learners learn? (4) What does a teacher teach?

These questions suggest a three-phase program in the local church.

Question 1 might involve a session or series of sessions on understanding adults and human relationships. Films, games, book studies, and interviews with laymen or professionals could provide you with information. Role-playing and sensitivity training (under competent leadership) might help you see how you would be likely to function in various situations. You might be interested in these aspects: the persistent life concerns of individuals, the developmental tasks of adults, the influence of culture, the meaning of maturity, and so on.

A second phase of your program could include the teaching-learning process, relating to questions 2 and 3. Teaching under the eye of an experienced teacher is developmental. Such practice, based on some grasp of learning theory, with opportunity for evaluation, is one way to build teaching skills. You will be concerned, for instance, with developing approaches helpful to learning, practicing two-way communication, gathering information, fostering creative imagination and problem-solving, thinking about ways to use what you learn, and evaluating your procedures.

Phase 3 of such a program, related to question 4, could extend over many fields of study. But your main concern will probably be in two broad areas: those that concern all humanity and those that have special interest for Christians. In other words, psychology, sociology, and politics on the one hand; and Bible, theology, ethics, and church history on the other. You might be more interested in finding out about basic principles, central questions, and current issues than you would be in amassing a large store of facts or answers.

For example, What is man? is a central question today. Many areas of study have real contributions to make, but no complete, final solution. One writer, Wolfhart Pannenburg, sees man caught in tension between self-centeredness and openness to the world.[2] Man is aware of the future as no other creature is. Although one uses imagination and creativity in a struggle for mastery, he is still dependent upon his fellow humans. How can we reconcile these opposites?

Courses, seminars, and weekend workshops provided by the annual conference or local interdenominational programs, art and film festivals, and other training opportunities can broaden your skills and techniques. But perhaps none of these opportunities is available to you—either through your church or through nonchurch institutions. In such a case, your individual study may be your only chance for improving your capabilities.

The following books are sources for individual study. Bibliographies will lead you to further exploration:

The Dynamics of Discussion, by Dean C. Barnlund and

---

[2] In *What Is Man?* (Philadelphia: Fortress Press, 1970).

Franklyn S. Haiman. Houghton Mifflin, 1960.

Group Leadership and Democratic Action, by Franklyn S. Haiman. Houghton Mifflin, 1951.

Creative Procedures for Adult Groups, edited by Harold D. Minor. Abingdon Press, 1968.

New Ways for a New Day, by Harold D. Minor. Abingdon Press, 1965.

Group Life

Four Concerns of Group Life

How many persons are there in your group? Five? Ten? Twenty? Whatever the number, the learning potential can be multiplied by that number if each person is responsible for the learning in the group. If there are five persons in the group, plus you, then that group provides a theoretical potential of five "teachers" for *each* member.

This potential is seldom realized. This may, in many cases, be due to the fact that the class members themselves are not equippped to be of maximum help to one another.

Several years ago Jack Gibb sketched out what he called Four Modal Concerns in Group Development. These he listed under one-word designations of Acceptance, Data, Goals, and Controls. (See *T Group Theory and Laboratory Method,* edited by Leland P. Bradford, Gibb, and others; John Wiley & Sons, 1964) .

Acceptance he listed first because of his profound belief in the necessity of having people willing to learn to trust one another. Acceptance does not mean that a group of people all think exactly alike; it is not a warm, syrupy feeling of comfort. Acceptance of one another is the kind of understanding and predictability that makes it possible for a group to move on to the other concerns.

Data is the information needed. Sometimes learning is cognitive, resulting in a knowledge or an accumulation of facts brought into focus on a problem.

The third concern is that of *goals*. Every group has goals, whether stated, spelled out in a rigid constitution, or even unexpressed. Some element of objective the members hold in common binds them into a common group. And when groups tend to pull apart, usually the element of a common goal has been lost.

Controls is a label for the fourth concern of group development. Every group has to have some style of functioning, and this style is usually given solidity and durability in some manner. The object of controls is to assure the members that this group can be counted on to continue to work toward the commonly held goals of the members.

Perhaps you have noticed that the paragraphs above indicate a great concern for the needs and hopes of individuals within the group. A well-structured group is one that supports and releases the unique individuality of each one of its members. Gibb's point is that *many groups take up these concerns in the wrong order,* and in so doing, hammer the individual into subjection.

The newly formed group may set about first to determine its goals. This seems laudable. But until you know the other group members fairly well, what assurance do you have that the goals you so glibly spell out will meet the real needs of the majority of the members?

As a matter of fact, until you know the other group members, you can't even trust the information they bring.

But when you get to know the other persons, you place their information in the perspective of your knowledge of them, and then it makes sense. Even though you may not agree with them you can understand why they say it.

One task you have as the leader of a group is to help it become basically an accepting group. You can best help equip the group members to be responsible for the life and work of the group by helping them to know one another, by quietly seeing that ideas do not take pre-eminence over human beings, and by giving time to the exploration of individual differences of perspective.

You can also help them trust one another if you trust them. If they learn from you, they can learn to trust one another, and then they will find that the other concerns of data, goals, and controls will fall into place.

Leadership Styles

The leader of an adult study group has the potential of several styles of leadership at his command. A chart of these leadership styles, ranging from most autocratic to most democratic, shows the relationship between each style and group freedom.

In the chart below the more autocratic styles of leadership are shown at the left, the more democratic styles at the right. The vertical distance *above* the diagonal line indicates the amount of leader authority with each style; the distance *below* the line indicates the amount of group freedom.

The leader who "tells" the group members what to do is comparable to the military type of leader who gives orders and commands that are to be obeyed without question. Precise obedience is drilled into the recruits so that in time of battle they will follow orders without question. Men are willing to accept this form of leadership when personal survival depends upon it.

The leader who "sells" his group an idea or approach is like a corporation president who gathers "yes men" around him. He identifies the problem; he decides on a course of action; he calls in his vice presidents and then proceeds to sell them the idea. If they know what is good for them, they "buy" his proposal.

Moving on toward the democratic end of the scale, we find the type of leader who may identify a problem and select an approach to its solution, which he then "tests" on the members. They are free to work it over, even modify and perfect it. This type of leader is willing to accept the group members' modifications as the proposal is put into action.

A leader who "consults" his group identifies the problem to be solved and then calls the others in, and they consider together the possible courses of action to be taken. When they have agreed on one, he puts the plan into effect.

The type of group leader who "joins" is willing for any group member to identify problems (without his having to do it), propose solutions, and set up courses of action. His function is to make sure that the decision reached is truly the will of all the group. The earlier the various members are used in the process of identifying and solving problems the more democratic a group is.

Incidentally, the word *problem* may seem a little strange when used in connection with an adult study group. But a moment's reflection will reveal the fact that a need to learn can be broken into a series of problems, such as, What needs do I have? What information must I have to work at those needs? Where will I put it into action? Any study group is a problem-solving group.

When a group member is concerned with realizing his maximum God-given potential, he will be content only with leadership that gives him maximum freedom within the group. Therefore a good group leader should try to move from the left toward the right end of the chart.

Autocratic

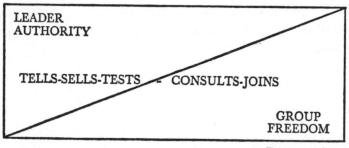

Democratic

In leading adult study groups, one is easily trapped into moving the wrong way on this chart. Consider this illustration:

Bill is the leader of a group of about twenty young married adults. His style could be located in about the middle of the chart. When the class finishes a unit, he looks over the possibilities for the next unit and *tests* out his ideas on the group at the next session. They work it over, suggest several modifications, but essentially go along with his basic suggestions.

However, as they move into the unit of study, Bill becomes concerned about apathy developing in the group. He feels that this is evidence that he is not exercising strong leadership, and so he moves toward the left on the chart. In the next session, for instance, he may select a unit *he* knows he can do well, and proceed to sell them on selecting his choice of a unit. But if he does this, even *more* apathy may very well follow because the group members will not be even remotely involved in the planning.

Bill's problem is that the group's apathy grew because none of the units he proposed really got at present needs of the class. If he had moved to the right on the chart, he would have had a greater chance of moving the group toward involvement in a real concern, and increased motivation.

Leadership Analysis

When adults meet together for study, each person carries responsibility for the growth and development of the group individually and collectively. Leadership is being defined more as a function than a role; each person in the group may at some time perform the leadership function.

This does not mean that many groups lack designated leaders, but it does say that each person must fulfill his responsibilities to the group if the greatest results are to be realized.

When any group comes together, two kinds of functions should be central in the operation of the group. One of these is the responsibility to each member, which is called group maintenance; and the other is the task function. How do you analyze the performance of a group?

Analyzing Group Maintenance Functions

People are important. A concern for the persons in the group may be overlooked because of the urgency of the task and the need to arrive at a decision. Since the group members must implement the decision and bring about the results of the decision, it is important to be aware of what is happening to them.

The productivity of a group may be heightened or lessened according to the way in which persons are treated and the way in which they feel they are being treated. Studies have shown that persons learn most when they feel they are accepted and are making a worthwhile contribution.

Any group that is concerned about maximum growth must make provision for consistent evaluation of the group's functioning. One way is by a device called the PMR.

Post meeting reaction sheets may be used periodically by a group to give some indication of how the group maintenance is being perceived. Such items as these might be used:

Did we really listen to one another?

Did we help others say what they wanted to say?

Did a few persons make all the suggestions and decisions?

Did you feel that you were a part of the group? Describe the ways you did or didn't.

This kind of group analysis should bring into focus the real feelings of the group members and the way they perceived what was going on. It is wise not to have the members sign the sheets. The responses could be tabulated and a report made to the group at the beginning of the next meeting. The use of a group observer—described on page 27—would be one way of getting some information immediately rather than waiting for the next meeting.

Task Performance

Most groups are highly task-oriented. The commitment to a group is often made on the basis of the particular task or purpose that the group has been formed to carry out. A check sheet at the end of a meeting would enable the members to see how well they functioned in relation to their task. Such questions as the following could be used: How well did we achieve our task?

What aided us in decision-making?

What were some hindrances we encountered?

How might we have worked more efficiently?

In some situations it will be wise to have a few members of a leadership team free to look more objectively at what is going on. Some meetings may be saved by injecting such comments as these:

"I wonder where we are in our discussion/decision?"

"I sense that we are not clear as to what our specific task is."

"I would like someone to tell me where he thinks we are at this point."

When a designated leader takes all the responsibility for a group and makes his own analysis of the task and the group's performance, it will be very difficult for him to make an objective analysis. He will be so emotionally involved that he will be unable to look at the way his behavior has affected the actions of the group. A reminder: under the concept of shared leadership, any group member is eligible to make comments like those above.

Any group can improve its ability to function effectively if it is willing to take the time to make an analysis of its performance—and then build future meetings on the basis of this evaluation.

Some evaluative instrument to check how the group sees its operation should be a built-in part of every learning experience. A project that extends over a period of six weeks to three months might include three evaluations.

Group Observer

For the group that is wanting to improve its effectiveness, a group observer is *a must*. It is almost impossible for a group to be objective about itself if all the members are continually involved as participants.

Role of the Group Observer

The observer sits outside the participating group and observes what is going on. He is not permitted to make a contribution to the group as long as he is in the observer role unless the group calls on him for a report. The group may do this at times throughout the session, or the observer may report at the end of the session what he saw and heard. The observer's role is not that of an evaluator in terms of his feelings and what "he thought"; rather, he must be as objective as possible and deal only with what he definitely saw and heard. He is an observer of the *group,* not an evaluator of individual behavior.

The observer may be asked to make a report on the distribution of member participation in the session. In fulfilling this assignment, he would keep a record of times each person spoke. (Often group members may have the feeling that everyone is participating, but when a count is made, they discover that very few were actually involved.) In reporting to the group, the observer would say, "One person spoke twenty times; one, twelve; one only once; and three did not speak at all."

Group members must look at this information to discover what it says about the functioning of their group and what, if anything, needs to be done to improve the situation. The group observer may be asked to note specific factors that are aiding the group in the achievement of their task and those that are hindrances. When the report is called for, the observer may report that the group spent a long time trying to make some "operational decisions," such as who would be the secretary, whether to serve tea or punch, or when they should meet again. The observer might indicate how much of the total time was spent in these nonfunctional activities. Considerable time may have been spent trying to identify the purpose of the meeting, when advance publicity could have made this clear.

On some occasions, the group observer will report that a group ceased to function because of some blocking roles performed by group members, such as playboy, attention getter, blocker.

Member Roles

If groups are to perform effectively, a variety of roles must be performed by the members. The group observer may be asked to look for such roles as initiating, asking questions, providing information, clarifying, summarizing, facilitating, and to report the various roles performed.

An analysis of the report can assist the group in recognizing some roles that members must assume if their group is to function effectively. Though the observer does not identify the members by name, a person who has been functioning primarily as an opinion-giver may see the need to get more facts. Group members who have been failing to "open the gate" (provide an opportunity for the more timid members to get into the discussion) may become more sensitive to one another and encourage each person to make a contribution.

Learnings for the Observer

The observer has the opportunity to sit outside the group and look at it from a detached position. He also gets a look at himself in a way he would not if he were always involved with the group. He is able to see himself through the behavior of other persons. He has an opportunity to see what group members can do to one another and their task. This should increase his productivity as a group member.

If a group has twenty to thirty persons, two, three, or four of them might be given the role of group observers. Each might be assigned a different aspect of group performance to observe.

Ample time should be given to the observer's report. It is most helpful when the group members have an opportunity to ask the observer some questions regarding his observations. (These should follow his complete report.) For a group that is taking seriously its responsibility for its members, it is imperative to have a person serving in the observer role. He sees and hears things that a group is unaware it is doing. For the growth of all members, the role of observer should be rotated.

Methods of Social Influence

As a result of your reading you may begin to wish to make some changes in your group work. You may wish to involve the class more deeply in determining its future work. Another wish may be to equip the members more adequately to "teach one another."

But how does one go about this? You cannot go in next week and order them to become responsible. You cannot insist that they become concerned about one another, and make it happen.

Your goal is to encourage others to make changes in their lives. Note how different this is from saying, "Your goal is to change others' lives." In the former, the implication is that each person is really in charge of his own life. In the latter, the implication is that your responsibility is to manipulate someone into changes that he would not willingly make. You cannot afford to be trapped in the role of the manipulator. Every such effort defeats your larger objectives in an adult learning group.

It has been said that a desire to change another person is essentially a hostile desire. This statement is undoubtedly too broad and too sweeping to be totally true. But it contains enough truth that it should make us examine our own motives in teaching. The reason we attempt to change Bill or old Mrs. Smith or young Sandy Jones may be that we simply cannot stand them the way they are. But we know that the only meaningful changes adults make in their approach to life are the ones they choose to make.

How does one person influence another? The complexities of this question can be distilled into three approaches. Any time one person influences another to do something different, to think different thoughts, to accept different attitudes, the second person accepts the influence because of one of three possibilities or a combination of them.

First, the influencer may demand some kind of *com-*

pliance by exerting a threat. You as the leader may make a proposal to the members and persuade them to accept it by leveling a threat along with the proposal. For example, "I think we need more than thirty minutes for class time on Sunday morning. If we cannot devote at least forty-five minutes to serious study, you had just better look for another teacher." Threats involved in attempts at influence will block the path of this approach, as shown in the top part of the drawing.

Second, the influencer may persuade others to change because of *identification* with him. This is the classical "Do it for my sake" approach: "I think we need more than thirty minutes for class time on Sunday morning. Would you be willing to schedule forty-five minutes? I think if you would take my word for it, you might like it."

Third, the influencer may influence for change by helping others *internalize,* or feel, the need for a change that would help them to achieve *their* goals. For example, he may say, "I think we need more than thirty minutes for class time on Sunday morning. You are being frustrated in doing the work you have cut out for yourselves, because the lack of time cuts you off in the middle of your work."

In the *compliance* situation, note that the members' response is not to the *proposal*—but to the leader. Their response is used to remove the threat.

In working through *identification,* the leader again causes the group to respond positively to *him,* rather than to his proposal. This time the response is a positive one of attraction, shown by the bottom line.

Only when they *internalize,* do members actually respond to the proposal itself. This gives them the dignity of freedom to weigh the merits of the proposal and to make alternative suggestions.

Of course, most of us actually combine these various approaches: "I think we need more than thirty minutes for class time on Sunday morning. You are frustrated in achieving your goals because of lack of time, and so am I. I will feel compelled to quit unless you schedule more time. So why not give it a try, at least, for my sake?"

As you set about to encourage your group members to assume more responsibility, you can get best results if you allow them to "internalize" a proposal. If they see the merits of it, they will feel free to build on your suggestion. So make sure your proposal is worthy of consideration.

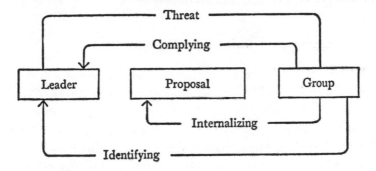

Sociograms

The sociogram is a graphic way of picturing the choices and feelings of a group. It grew out of the sociometric method developed to show the feelings of rejection and acceptance of persons and the ways these feelings influence group life.

The use of a sociogram may enable a group to use its time and resources with greater value. It can reveal who the members see as being the most influential, the ones they perceive as manipulators, outsiders, good listeners, and even those they see as blocking the group in the tasks it is attempting to perform.

The perceptions members have of one another have a great deal to do with the communication within a group and the group's ability to function. Persons do affect the behavior of others, and they are influenced both positively and negatively by the actions of others.

Using a Sociogram

When there is an open, honest, and trustful climate, group members will be more honest with one another and more objective about their behavior than if they are communicating in a superficial way. A sociogram might best be used with groups that make periodic inventories of their actions. If groups are accustomed to making evaluations concerning the roles that help and hinder their functioning, they can use a sociogram objectively.

Since persons do affect one another, sometimes the composition of a group may be such that the persons have reached an impasse and the possibility for growth is almost nil unless group memberships are changed. Sometimes it is wise at the start of a project to let the members make some decisions about groupings. This could be done best in groups whose members know one another by face and name. Questions such as the following might be asked:

If you were going to be involved in a study project with some members of this group, who would you like to have in your group?

If you were to undertake a difficult work project, what person would you like to have assist you?

If you were facing a very difficult personal problem, what persons would you like to be near you?

If you were going to spend an informal afternoon of fun and relaxation, who would you like to have share it with you?

Answers to such questions will indicate the persons who exert a great deal of influence on the group and those who exert very little. On the basis of responses to such questions as those above, groups may be named to work together.

In one adaptation of the sociogram such questions as the following might be asked:

—Who are the most influential members of your group?

—Who initiates decision-making?

—Who are the listeners?

—Who is helping the group move toward the desired goal?

—Do any members seem unclear about the group's purpose?

In answering any of these questions the person may list as many names as he wishes. In each case he will need to include his name on the paper. When the responses are charted, they may look something like the drawing on this page.

Questions that will indicate the way in which the persons see *themselves* could also be helpful.

—Do you see yourself as being important to this group?
—Do persons listen when you speak?
—Do you feel you influence the group?

Using a sociogram is a good way to discover how members are feeling about one another and themselves. It offers the possibility of restructuring the group in ways that may lead to more meaningful membership and greater productivity.

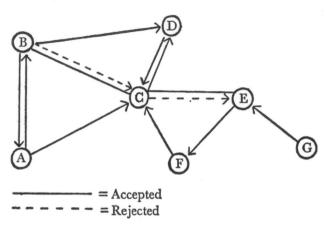

———————— = Accepted
— — — — — — = Rejected

Personal Dimensions in a Group

Fight

The middle-class culture in which the church is caught rewards ideas but punishes feelings. As a result, we tend to deal with anger or conflict in irrational ways.

A teacher of adults who attempts to use group discussion procedures is likely to find persons in his groups who respond to uncertainty—about leadership, their membership in that group, ethical or theological standards—by arguing, disagreeing, "fighting." This may be the only method a person has learned to use in coping with situations of stress.

A teacher will probably respond most helpfully to a "fighting" person:

If he is aware of his own tendencies to fight.

If he is aware of his emotional response to a "fight" person or conflict situation.

If he can support the person in such a way that that person can continue to be honest.

If he can help the person find other behaviors that are confronting but also more supportive.

If he can remember that some persons come into a situation in a fighting mood.

If he can listen both to the words of the person who is fighting and to his expression of emotion.

If he can sometimes respond to the ideas being expressed by the fighting person and at other times to the emotion.

In fact, the person fighting probably has not taken time to learn anything about the leader. Thus if he directs his hostility toward the leader, the chances are that he is more concerned with his own problems than with problems involving the leader. One way to check this out is to ask a person who is hostile toward you what you did that made him angry. If he can tell you specific things, you may learn something about your own behavior. But if he only says, "I don't know—I just get that feeling," more than likely he is dealing almost exclusively with his own problem.

If the leader is comfortable with an open facing of angry feelings in a group, he can say to the fighting person, "Fred we're having difficulty communicating because you seem so angry. Tell me—are you angry with me?" Fred may not be aware of his anger. Indeed, he may report that he is not angry even though he looks angry. If the leader considers it important, he might check it out with others and say something like this: "Was I the only one who thought Fred was angry?" If Fred denies being angry, the leader can smooth the situation over by saying, "O.K. I thought you were angry, but you say you are not. This puzzles me, but let's go on."

Expression of emotion makes many leaders and members so uncomfortable they try to suppress it. One way they do this is to deny that emotion is involved (for example, "He isn't angry, he's just expressing an opinion"). Another is to end the meeting early ("Perhaps we had better quit for now and try our luck again another day"). Still another way is to change the subject.

Part of the resistance to facing anger openly and talking about it when it occurs comes from the fear that such an openness may take the lid off a Pandora's box of human ills and free other emotions for expression in the group.

When emotions are suppressed, this suppression tends to use up the energy of the persons so that they cannot grasp concepts and discuss ideas rationally. Anxious, frustrated, angry persons and persons with low self-esteem have reduced energy, and thus decreased ability, for coping with important issues. The ability to work is directly affected by emotionality.

Flight

People feel, and people think. Our culture tends to reward thinking but to ignore or punish expression of feelings. A heated discussion is considered by many as "bad." Often adults hide their true feelings. But it is hard to get to know another person if you do not know how he feels. It is hard for another person to get to know you if you will not share with him what you care deeply about, what bothers you, excites you, frightens you, engages you.

Observe persons talking about the college riots or the war in Vietnam, and their words may indicate that these are entirely rational issues. However, their tone of voice, their ability or inability to look you in the eye, their nervous actions and bodily tension, and their facial expression may confirm that they care deeply even though they may try not to show it.

One way persons in a group avoid struggling with their own personal values and avoid conflict with others is by taking flight: they attempt to keep the conversation objective and rational, dealing with theories and generalities rather than with personal matters. Clergy may take flight by discussing theology, psychologists by discussing psychology, laymen by discussing sports, women by discussing children. All these can be seen as ways of preserving unity in the group and of avoiding conflict.

When you avoid conflict, however, you probably also avoid learning. But certain responses can be made by leaders to enable flight through theorizing to be constructive.

The leader probably can be most helpful in a flight situation—that is, in his response to a person who theorizes a lot—under these conditions:

The leader himself is aware of his own tendencies to flight.

He is aware of his emotional response (his dislike or fondness) to a person who quotes a lot or spins a lot of theories.

He supports the person who is theorizing in such a way that he can continue to theorize but in a manner that helps the group understand its own life experience.

He remembers that some persons use theorizing as a way of avoiding personal involvement. If the theorizing is flight, probably few others will participate and most of the group will be bored.

The leader can respond by calling attention to the low participation and saying something like this: "I wonder if the low participation also means low interest. To check this out, pick a partner or two and talk about how you feel about our discussion today—what you've liked most and what you've liked least. Then I'd like for us to discuss this in the total class."

This assignment gives the low participators an easy group in which to talk (with one or two others). Beware the leader who would ask the group's advice before making this assignment, for the answer would probably come from the active, high participators who would say, "It has been very interesting, and we *don't* need to pair off and discuss this."

Theorizing, working on abstract notions, is important. It only becomes flight when it is used to avoid real personal learning.

Theorizing is most likely to help persons face their situation when—

1. It is an attempt to explain some experience the per-

sons in the group have had or an experience that has just happened in the group.

2. It uses other resources, but has as its primary resource the feelings and observations of the person theorizing.

3. It uses illustrations that all or most of the group have experienced.

4. It is presented as one way to organize or understand what is being discussed or experienced.

5. It is brief—to the point.

Dependency and Pairing

Some persons feel a need to be related to someone who can give them direction. ("What are we supposed to do?" "You've led these groups before, but this is my first time, so tell me what you've done before." "Well, you're the teacher, aren't you?") They want the leader to take charge. If the leader chooses to do this by placing goal-setting, resource-scanning, or discussion leadership in the hands of the learners (even with occasional brief lectures by the leader), he is accused of inept leadership because this is not the "take charge" behavior usually expected.

A teacher whose exclusive style is lecturing probably meets the need on which W. R. Bion based this assumption: "The group has met together to obtain security from one individual on whom they depend." [1]

If the leader's style does not fulfill the group's dependency needs and expectations, the group members may respond with fight or flight behavior. A leader can help such a group by having the members list their expectations

[1] *Experience in Groups* (New York: Basic Books, 1961), p. 66.

of the leader and the ways in which he has and has not met their expectations. This should enable the group to begin focusing on the central issue, which may be their unrealistic and unhealthy dependency on the leader.

Dependency may also take the form of disagreeing with everything the leader says or does. This is defeating, for even though the leader does not know everything, he *does have valuable resources.*

The goal in the leader-member relationship is interdependency, each recognizing a need for the other without turning over his learning to the other. Persons bring to a group a lifetime of group and school experience in which they have depended on a leader, and this creates an expectation of dependency. On the other hand, many leaders and teachers "need" to keep people dependent on them; at least they don't have the courage or skill to face the hostile feelings that would come if they tried to break the dependent leader-group relationship.

Bion mentions another way that persons often respond to a confused and uncertain situation—"pairing." Whispering in the classroom is one evidence of "pairing"—it is easier to deal with one other person than the whole class. Eventually, pairing behavior becomes unsatisfactory to the individuals because: (*a*) they notice that they are being watched; (*b*) they are not sure but that they are using, or are being used by, the other person in the pair; (*c*) they begin to suspect that they are being a disruptive force in the group.

Actually, pairing can be very supportive. A person who might not otherwise speak up can get encouragement to do so by checking his idea with somebody in the group. A teacher might make use of pairing in these ways:

1. Building pairings into the regular class structure. For instance, he might invite pairing midway in the class session by saying, "Talk for five minutes with someone of your choice about what you are thinking or feeling right now in this class."

2. Encouraging more small group work in the class, giving dependent persons more support than is being given by the total class.

Emotional responses such as fight, flight, dependency, and pairing are present in all kinds of groups. These responses are not bad—they are facts of life that affect the work and life of any group. Rather than ignoring them, we need to face the issue: What can be done to work with, rather than against, the presence of emotion in problem-solving groups?

If a major purpose of the group is to help individuals understand themselves, it would be helpful for those persons to learn how to talk about these emotional dimensions. It is likely that these dimensions in the group reflect the development of the individual members when they are in this group, in their family, and in many other groups. Self-understanding of their response in your group may help them understand themselves in other situations.

Conflict and Controversy

Conflict and *controversy*. Those dread words have echoed around church corridors like a clap of thunder on doomsday. What leader of an adult group has not had to think about this problem? The result of most such thought is a determination to find ways to prevent, or at least minimize, such struggle.

Perhaps a fresh look is in order. Four current conditions suggest it:

1. Many adult learning groups in churches have a well deserved reputation for being bland, dull, unstimulating. A vast number of church members avoid participation in such groups.

2. Members of these classes often go to extremes to avoid disagreeing with one another in class, yet *outside* the classroom will express disagreement at what was agreed upon.

3. This insistence upon agreement at almost any cost forces the members of learning groups to betray their own integrity.

4. When hot, aggressive argument does break out in such a group, it usually produces heat but little light; it frightens people; and it causes things to be said that hurt and estrange members.

What can the leader of the learning group do about conflict? First, a brief study of the four factors above shows a causal relationship. Number 4 occurs *because of* (not despite) numbers 2 and 3. Thus the ideal that is sought (a conflict-free group) tends to produce number 1.

You will find this a more fruitful approach: If differences of viewpoint are accepted, and if expressions of these differences are encouraged, then people will start to express themselves *in* the class, instead of outside it. Such expression will give them a sense of integrity. This gives those who are expressing the differences a sense of support, a sense of acceptance, which allows them to relax—even in the presence of their differences. And in the process, they give far more careful attention to the perspective of the other person, thereby growing in their understanding.

Conflict, while widely feared in learning groups, need not be destructive. Some forms of conflict are destructive, of course. But other forms are neutral—neither good nor bad. And still other forms are enjoyable, exciting, and appealing. Perhaps some analysis is in order.

All forms of conflict flow out of two types of social situations that are sometimes referred to as *distributive* and *integrative*. One common characteristic is that persons in both situations are in some kind of social system together. For example, if no contact were made between parents, they would never be in conflict.

Distributive conflict grows out of the situation in which goods that are scarce have to be distributed among us. This distribution is such that if I get more, you get less; if you get more, I get less. This, then, becomes a win-or-lose situation. When persons are caught together in a win/lose situation, they tend to become cautious, secretive, insecure, and belligerent.

Integrative conflict, by contrast, occurs in those social situations in which if I win, you win too. And if you win, I win also. The friendly competition among members of a ball team is a good illustration of this kind of conflict. This situation, then, becomes a win/win setting.

A learning group can be sidetracked into a win/lose experience through such emotional traps as these:

"I didn't get to express my ideas today because Bill used all the time on his concerns."

"Thanks for the way you led out today, Bill. It sure was better than when Mike was in charge."

"We really showed 'em today, didn't we!"

But don't despair. A group that has worked on a win/ lose basis can re-educate itself into a win/win stance.

A learning group is an integrative social situation—not a distributive one. So the positive conflict of healthy interchange of opinions and ideas, the friendly competition to produce the clearest analysis of a situation, and the zest of determination to do the best job of leading the class in a discussion—all these are forms of conflict that cause us all to win.

The Dominator

Most groups have one or more persons who tend to dominate the work of their group. You as a leader may have had to contend with this. Sometimes persons are so dominating that the leader hesitates to use the democracy of a discussion, fearing that it will be overcome by the overactive member.

Warren Schmidt and Gordon Lippitt have classified these persons into a number of types. You will find their analysis helpful, because the different types of persons call for different responses.

• The "enthusiastic over-participant" gets carried away by what is going on.

• The "insensitive dominator" does not notice that he is dominating.

• The "over-clarifier" fears that people do not understand him, so he keeps repeating himself, illustrating and clarifying his points.

• The "neurotic dominator" finds an outlet for intense personal needs in talking.

• And the "above-group-average dominator" feels that he must save the group from its own inadequacies.

Do not attempt to work on such a problem in your own group until you have a fair idea concerning your own motivation. For, as leader, you may find yourself threatened by this dominator. Not only does he tend to destroy the discussions you get started, but he even seems to challenge your leadership of the group.

You must remember that your aim is *not* to destroy him. And if these seem like strong words, recall that there are many ways of destroying another person: you can break his spirit by shaming him publicly, or you can treat him paternalistically—like a child. But none of these *redeem* his potential for group contribution or help him become more perceptive of his own needs.

Here are some suggestions that may give you some insights for dealing with a dominator:

• If he is an over-participant, you may be able to use his energies outside the classroom. This benefits the entire class.

• If he is insensitive to his dominating, a gentle but honest approach to him privately may cause him to become more aware of the feelings of others.

• If he is an over-clarifier or a neurotic dominator, you may well need to call on several other members of the class (privately, of course) to see how they can give him a sense of support and acceptance that allows him to relax a bit more in the classroom.

• If he is the above-group-average dominator, he will probably respond to your efforts to give him leadership responsibilities.

The objective of this work is not simply to keep the dominator busy, not simply to control him, but to make his potential available to the group and to himself. Each of us has potential, and each has limitations that block our potential. Your work with the dominator may be more obviously needed, but it is not too different from your work with other members. (For example, there is the "under-participant," who in his own way needs help to make available his contributions just as much as does the dominator.)

One other idea before closing out this topic: suppose—just suppose—that *you* are the dominator in your learning group. It is possible, you know. One oddity in this business is that if the dominator also happens to be the group leader, he is not so readily identifiable—in fact, he may be just living up to the group's expectations.

This says something about leadership, doesn't it? That people *expect* to be dominated by a leader. But this as surely blocks learning on the part of other members of the group as it would if the dominator were another member. The problem is just as big—bigger, really—because of the nature of the leader's role.

So give a little thought to this. Do you really make it possible for others to participate as they should? Do you really rejoice when the group members make contributions you were not able to make?

Guiding a Study Group

Equipping a Class for Teaching/Learning

A major shift has been introduced into adult curriculum approaches: The new thrust was in the direction of urging adults to assume more responsibility for their own learning. The logic for this emphasis can be shown in the following statements:

—Christian education is concerned with relating the gospel to the persistent life concerns of every person.

—No two people have the same environment, the same experiences.

—Thus no two people have the same persistent life concerns.

—Therefore a church can best educate adults by giving maximum opportunity for the persistent life concerns of each person to be recognized and studied in light of the gospel.

—Since no adult can be responsible for another's persistent life concerns, each adult should be responsible for his own learning.

Sometimes classes present a teacher with obstacles to work against in introducing changes. But the start of a new unit gives him opportunity for some new starts in a new direction.

Creating a Climate

How does one create a climate that stimulates a class to become responsible for its own learning? Rule number 1: *You as leader must be willing to get out of the way.*

A flood of objections and defenses may pour into your mind. But reflect on this idea for a moment: If you enjoy leading a group, there is the constant temptation to *use* the group for your own satisfaction. We all enjoy being needed, and we experience a very subtle pleasure in having a group of adults dependent on us. But we should recognize that in a number of ways we may unconsciously wish to keep the group dependent on us.

Take the simple matter of discussion. Very probably you do not lecture all through the hour, and you probably allow others to bring their concerns into consideration. But study the two diagrams below. If circles represent persons, and arrows show the flow of conversation during a discussion, which diagram would look most like *your* group?

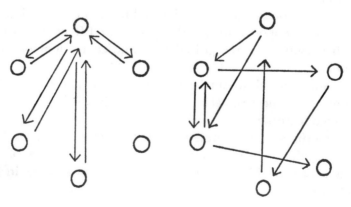

The left-hand diagram shows a discussion very much under the control of the leader. Instead of being a single discussion group, it is really a series of two-person groups, with the leader a part of each group. By contrast, the other diagram shows group members freely interacting with one another and learning from one another.

It is not easy to form this kind of group. Years of exposure to classes in school, college, and church have trained people to be dependent upon a teacher. Thus a simple desire on your part to back off and let them be more nearly responsible for their own learning will not necessarily produce the desired results. Very likely many of the members will feel threatened. They may wonder why you aren't willing to "teach" them. Efforts to get them involved in the leadership of the group will bring grumbling reactions to the effect that you are shirking your duty. Efforts to help the group be responsible for its own learning may bring pointed comments about "pooling of ignorance" and "camels are horses put together by committees."

In forming this kind of study group keep in mind rule number 2: *Groups that are responsible for the learning of each member are far more effective.*

The following pages contain suggestions for using the learning potential in your group.

The Steering Committee

You as a leader must feel a responsibility for creating an atmosphere in which each adult is partly responsible for his own learning. This is necessary because of the uniqueness of each individual's sum of experiences. Possibly this principle was not made clear when you agreed to teach. You may see yourself in much more traditional roles: lecturing, studying to be the expert, answering questions, inspiring loyalty, or attracting new members by the force of your personality.

Class members should be involved at the point of deciding what they will study. This will allow the studies to focus on the felt needs of the class members. They can decide on the focus, the materials, and their goals.

Or can they? Obviously, the plans made by the group at the beginning of a study unit will depend on their knowledge at that time. The changes that may occur cannot be seen or predicted at the beginning. It is possible for a unit to lose its challenging aspects simply because it is outlined on the basis of what little the group knew when the study was launched.

What can be done to prevent such a pitfall? One answer is in the use of a steering committee. This is a small group of persons within the larger group which meets briefly and often to evaluate, to check progress, to work out changes in direction—in short, to steer. The number of people on the steering committee should be kept small enough for frequent sessions to be arranged easily, with a minimum of three.

If your group has both men and women, and they seem very often to have different points of view, you would want both a man and a woman on the steering committee. If different age groups represent different points of view, have a representative from each age group. If several ongoing groups are coming together for one unit of study, have a representative from each of them.

Each member of the steering committee will need to have a copy of the overall picture of the study unit—how the group arrived at the decision to study this particular unit, what parts they emphasized, what resources were available within the group, and what supplementary resources they would use.

The steering committee can then meet for a short time following each session to appraise the direction the study is moving. During the sessions they can observe interest or apathy of the entire group or of individuals. They can also bring together their observations or the results of conversations with various class members.

As an example, let us say that an ongoing class that meets on Sunday morning decided to study "A Christian's Approach to Death." They launched the study after their class planning was completed. The steering committee decided to start by observing the group's reactions to the study. They became aware that one woman was not attending the sessions, although she was present at other functions. They learned that she was facing the loss of a family member in terminal illness and had found the study very painful. Yet a similar situation existed in the life of another member, who found it very meaningful to be with the group in the study. Awareness of such personal factors in the group helped the steering committee in their evaluations and planning.

As the study progressed, the steering committee realized they were delving into funeral practices. Some of the class members wanted to discuss funeral practices with all the funeral directors of the town; this idea was brought to the steering committee. The steering committee, late in the study, brought to the group the idea of this unit being used in a workshop setting for people who might sign up voluntarily to attend.

A look back at the original planning indicated how valuable the steering committee had been. Reflecting class progress and direction would have been difficult for one person to do alone.

Planning Assignments

The purpose of assignments is to expose class members to a body of information that might become the basis for sharing or discussion, for the old saying is often true that classroom discussion is a "pooling of ignorance," especially if the groups have not done the necessary background reading. It is important for each person to have a copy of the book, article, or other material to be read and studied. He can then gauge his own time for study and reflection without feeling under pressure. The knowledge gained in this way should serve as a stimulus for creative, objective thinking.

Early Arrivers

Assignments can be made during the teaching-learning session. Early arrivers might be asked to review additional resource materials in books, short articles in encyclopedias, and so on. These people might also note and prepare to discuss during the class period any displays, charts, graphs, books, and art work around the room. Or a filmstrip to be shown during the session might be previewed by early arrivals. This means that the audiovisual equipment should be ready, and it means also that these persons will have two viewings. These viewers may start the discussion or reaction to the filmstrip later in the session.

A very good teaching method for adult classes (particularly if persons arrive at different times) is to have one or more discussion questions considered by small groups of four to six as members arrive. The first four can be given questions typed on index cards and then asked to discuss the questions in a circle. The next four to six people who arrive can form another group—with either the same questions or different ones—until the whole class is present.

This method often separates persons who tend to sit together, and gives them an opportunity to know others. In so doing they have a sense of involvement and participation from the time they arrive. It is important to call for a report from each group on their discussion of at least one question during the session. This planned assignment prompts people to think, talk, share, and listen. Further, learning can take place, and barriers between persons can begin to break down. When this happens, acceptance and mutual appreciation take place among people, and the climate for Christian growth is improved.

Another suggestion is that class members be divided into small groups during the session and given a topic to discuss and present to the total group at the end of the session or at the beginning of the next session. For example, in a consideration of the Apostles' Creed, class members could be asked to choose one of the following exploration groups: (1) origin and history, (2) translation in today's language, (3) parts that are "stumbling blocks" for today's churchmen, (4) interpretation of its meaning section by section. This assignment, in order to be effectively handled, might require that the small groups meet one day during the week.

One page of mimeographed materials or a short article can be assigned for all to read at the beginning of a class session. In this way each person has the same knowledge immediately at hand on which to base his opinions and ideas.

Outside Research

Additional excitement and enthusiasm for a unit of study can be stimulated by carefully choosing individuals to do outside research for class sharing at a later session. Individuals who make little contribution during a session may be stimulated by an outside assignment in a particular field or area that they are interested in pursuing. Their renewed interest may have a good influence on other class members.

Between-session assignments need not always be reading but might include interviewing persons for beliefs and opinions, watching and reporting on a television program or motion picture, making a poster, or doing research in an interesting field related to the unit of study. Some assignments may be completed in one week, while others may require a longer period of time.

The teacher must prepare for every assignment and make it relevant to the study. He must always seek to arouse interest in the subject and give the assignee a chance to present his results to the group. The class member puts in his own words the results of his outside work and in so doing becomes a teacher and witness. The teaching-learning process is then truly fulfilled.

A Task Force Approach

A task force is a group of "units" drawn together for the specific accomplishment of a particular task. It is composed of those units necessary for the task, and no others. It has no continuing life of its own; when the task is finished, the task force disbands.

Several convictions are necessary among the members of a learning group before they can organize along these lines.

1. A learning group makes a difference to its members; education has consequences; and people *do* change.

2. A group can and should be a "mover and shaker." That is, it must also change the environment in which the members find themselves.

3. The members should bind themselves together for the purpose of action, rather than leave it up to each individual to act alone.

If a learning group has these convictions, the studies pursued will generate an educated determination to make changes in their situation.

When, as a result of class studies, one or more of the members feels compelled to swing into action, this action should be the responsibility of the class just as much as the study itself. For example, it may happen that the studies about conditions in the days of Amos cause two of your class members to say, "I wonder if things are so different in our town today? I'd like to find out." The class, in effect, then "commissions" these two interested persons as a task force to set out in pursuit of the answer.

The class helps these two clarify their task. One of the other class members might say, "But I don't see what you are going to do. There were poor people and injustices in Amos' day. There are still some of each. So what?" Another member chimes in: "That's not the point. The point is that the ethical decisions of persons in a community have social consequences. These decisions should be influenced by Christian values."

One of the two task force members responds: "It seems to me that we are really looking for evidence of a correlation between religious faith and ethical conduct." And the other task force member: "Then we have some homework to do before we go into the community. We have to figure out how to go about this. You and I had better get together sometime this week, work out some proposals, and report to the class next week."

Thus, as a result of some group study, a small task force is "briefed" and sent out to do its work. At subsequent class sessions, the same task force reports the information it has received.

Another illustration is provided when a group discussion leads some members to the conviction that action is needed in the community. They set out as a task force, not simply to get more information, but to *act*. As a result of the action and reports, further steps may be decided upon. In this manner the class moves into a very healthy pattern of planning, action, and evaluation, followed by more planning, more action, and so on.

Education is not simply the acquisition of more knowledge. It is a dynamic interaction between knowledge, attitudes, and behavior. The action phase of any study is as real a part of the education as is the intellectual phase. Study without action in the form of some changed behavior or attitudes is a sterile exercise; action without study is purposeless milling about.

This leads one to the conclusion that adult education is *not* primarily what happens for an hour a week during your class session; rather it is what happens during the week *as a result of* that hour. The task force approach to adult learning is one way to take advantage of this principle.

The class members come together to assess the problem, select their assignment, and form their task forces. Then they scatter for the week, singly or in groups, to work on their assignments. Later they come back together to be debriefed.

59

The Systems Approach to Learning

A new approach to dealing with highly complex problems has been developed in recent years. It is called the systems approach. It was initially developed to be used by planners in technological fields such as air and space.

The systems approach begins when a company, a group, or individuals need to solve a problem or accomplish a task. In using the systems approach the first task is to identify the major parts of the total task. These separately identifiable tasks make up the several *systems* that feed in to make the total goal achievable. In considering a moon trip, for example, the systems might include a flight vehicle system, a booster system, a communications system, a life support system, a power system, a ground control system, a crew training system, and so on. Each aspect of the whole complex trip is worked on separately. A team of experts then coordinates the whole project to ensure that the finished program is workable.

Systems analysis is an adaptation of this planning procedure. Given a certain interest or concern, one way to understand the issue is to identify all the related parts, or *systems,* that affect it or give it its meaning.

Suppose your task is to explore the roots of the generation gap in our day. You might begin by looking first at the younger generation. But it will quickly become apparent that there are many systems relating to this issue that one needs to examine: one's son or daughter, young adults in your church, the hippies, college students who participate in demonstrations, college students who avoid demonstrations, young servicemen, young employed persons, unemployed persons, and so on.

Looking at the older side of the gap, one sees such systems as fathers and mothers, businessmen, clergymen, university administrators, draft board members, policemen, senior executives, politicians, retired (yet still active) military leaders, and so on.

Try a different illustration of the process of systems analysis, such as a systems analysis of the violence at the Democratic Convention in Chicago in 1968. Instead of just listing the systems, you might chart them in a manner somewhat like the diagram below.

You can see that by making such an analysis of the various contributing factors behind an event, a problem, or a task, one has before him enough information to work with an awareness of the whole task. This approach has the advantage of helping one discover that "simple" matters often are indeed quite complex.

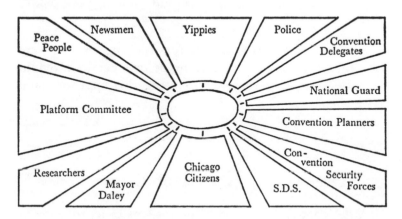

Here is another illustration: Suppose your problem is to lead a group in compiling a specific list of things to be done to help the poor in a nearby area. What systems do you need to explore in order to bring back a list of suggestions? What tasks would be genuinely useful and not designed just to make the helpers feel good?

One writer has evaluated this method in the following manner:

> Dealing with the mythology of systems analysis requires making a distinction as delicate as that between ultimate promise and immediate possibility. The myth of systems analysis holds that educational salvation lies in applying to education the planning and control techniques commonly believed to have been successful in the defense and aerospace industries. Advocating systems analysis as a panacea [universal solution] ranks with making the world safe for democracy, unconditional surrender, and massive retaliation as an experiment in delusion for political ends. Yet, not to believe in the usefulness of systems analysis is to deny the value of reason, common sense, and, indeed, the scientific method.[1]

Systems analysis is a process for studying any problem or preparing for any task. It helps one get involved in learning. Guide your group in using this approach, and try it soon.

Overcoming Barriers of Expectation

A designated leader has a first responsibility to discover the expectations of the group he is to lead. Why are these

[1] Anthony G. Oettinger, "The Myths of Educational Technology," *Saturday Review*, May 18, 1968, p. 77.

persons there? What do they anticipate will happen because they have given their time and energy to prepare for and attend this particular session?

Setting Goals

If the leader and the group are to arrive at a previously determined destination, then both must participate in setting goals. Persons are usually willing to work for the goals they have helped to select, but they may be very apathetic in the pursuit of someone else's goals. When goals are not clearly set and understood by those involved in the learning process, it is impossible for them to assess accurately whether or not they have made or are making progress in achieving those goals.

Some groups may need to use the first meeting or two to identify the goals they wish to achieve. These may relate to the knowledge they wish to gain, the appreciations they wish to deepen, the attitudes they wish to broaden, the behavior they wish to change.

In some groups goal-setting may involve the total group. Other groups may divide into smaller work units and later share with the total group their expectations of the learning enterprise. Again, the designated leader may ask several group members to meet with him ahead of time to help set goals in the light of their own expectations. These goals could be proposed to the total group at the regular session.

A group rarely arrives at significant learnings by chance. Some very significant "side" learnings may come about in the process of pursuing desired goals—but without some goal determination, these learnings probably would not occur. When the expectations of the group members can be brought to the fore and used as a focus for direction, the experience will have much more value for them than will aimless study or action.

Group members need help in being able to speak honestly and openly with one another within the learning situation. When the study is moving contrary to their expectations, they need to indicate this in a helpful manner to the leader and other group members, especially if there is a real possibility of changing the situation to be more in line with achievement of their goals.

At times the designated leader may need to introduce some material or procedure that may not meet with an enthusiastic group response. But if the members can see why this change is necessary in the light of their stated expectations, they can usually accept it. No one likes to feel that another person is manipulating him. We like to know why certain things are being done, and a group and its leader need to have a common understanding at this point.

Assessing the Results

Unless groups and leaders have taken time to set goals and to plan the course of action, they will be unable to make any evaluation as to whether or not the desired ends have been achieved.

Perhap two main shortcomings of groups are (1) their failure to set clear, specific, achievable goals in the light of the expectations; and (2) their failure to make an evaluation at the end of an experience to see what was accomplished and how. The comment, "We learn to do by doing," is more accurately stated, "We learn from our evaluated doing." What helped in the achievement of the goals? What hindered? What might have been done differently? How do the results of the work measure up to the expectations? If we begin again with the same set of expectations, what should we do differently?

At the heart of the church is concern for persons. Therefore, the teaching-learning situation will be set up to discover the expectations of the adults and to aid them in the achievement of these expectations.

The concerned learning group will (1) find out the expectations of the persons involved; (2) set goals accordingly; (3) make a periodic check to see if the movement is in the direction of the goals; and (4) evaluate the learnings at the end of the study against the expectations set by the potential learners. When such a procedure is followed, each later learning opportunity should be more meaningful.

Overcoming Barriers of Language

Because persons speak a common language are they able to communicate with one another? While a common language and culture may enhance the ability to communicate more accurately, there is no guarantee that such will be the case. In recent years many conferences and workshops have been held on the subject of communication, and numerous articles and books have been written on it.

Some feel the inability to communicate accurately and honestly with individuals and nations is a problem of primary importance. It will surely increase as we move into a more complex, specialized, and computerized twenty-first century.

Difficulties in Communication

When any group of individuals come together—whether husband and wife, parent and child, or a larger number of persons—each brings with him his own understandings, his own experiences, his own images, his own perceptions. Therefore, when words are spoken, the receiver must decode them in light of his understanding and seek to make sense out of them. The more perfectly he is able to decode the message intended by the sender, the greater the accuracy in the communication.

Words do not have meaning in and of themselves: people give meaning to the words. Each brings his own meanings, his own interpretations, to the words he hears, and he reacts to them in the light of his own unique experience.

In *The Miracle of Dialogue* Reuel Howe speaks of communication as the "meeting of meaning." Unless the spoken words can convey to the listener some meaning intended by the sender, there has been no communication. Often we do not know what meaning the words we have spoken have carried to the receiver. We assume that because a certain word has a certain meaning to us, it will have a similar meaning to another. The only way we can be sure is to test to see what the meanings are.

For example, if you are beginning a unit of study on

such a subject as the church, situation ethics, or theology, it would be good at the very first session to find out something of what these words mean to those who are to participate in the study. Unless we take time at the very beginning of a series to make certain that our bases for work and study are somewhat comparable, we may go through several seeks of study but never arrive at the meeting of meanings Reuel Howe refers to.

Test Meanings

Any group can test word meanings in at least two very simple ways: (1) find out what the word or the theme means to individual members, and (2) find out what the words mean to the group.

Perhaps more often than we would admit, we talk in order to influence someone else, to bring him around to our point of view. When this takes place, the sender is more intent on what he is trying to get the other to do or think than in what the other is actually hearing and experiencing.

When the sender is concerned with the meaning the receiver grasps, he will be interested in knowing how his words have been received. He will seek some feedback. Encouraging receivers to state what they thought they heard the speaker saying is one way of testing to make sure that what the speaker thought he conveyed was what the receiver actually heard.

Each person carries responsibility to facilitate communication each time a group comes together. Group members need to be encouraged to say to one another and to the leader, "Is this what you said . . . ?" or "I heard you saying . . ."

When the person receiving a message is able to restate it to the sender's satisfaction, then one can be assured he has received the thoughts of the speaker. This is a simple way of testing how clearly and accurately we are hearing each other. How much headache and heartache could be avoided by rechecking the meanings we receive with the intended meanings of the sender!

Sensing Deficiencies of Knowledge

Before a person can learn he must want to learn. He must want to know, to discover, to change, or it will be very difficult, if not impossible, for him to change.

How does one become aware of deficiencies in his knowledge to the degree that he is moved to do something about it?

Man struggles with a deep sense of his own inferiority, often for reasons that are very minor and ill-founded, yet which are real for him and he therefore acts upon them. What might be done to help him decrease these deficiencies he feels and hence aid him in moving into a more confident role?

The group of which he is a member may be helpful at this point. When a group is open, honest, and trusting, members find it easier to expose themselves than to cover up their deficiencies. A person will rarely "show his face" if he feels inferior in a group that is nonaccepting, judg-mental, and does not communicate to him that he is of worth. Every person is eager to have others think well of him. Therefore he does not like to let on he does not "know," for fear this will destroy any favorable image held by those who know him. A caring, supportive, open, and trusting group would be necessary in moving from de-ficiency in knowledge to efficiency.

Deficiencies in knowledge could be discovered as a new unit of study is started. For example, through activities used in the opening session the leadership team or the designated leader might find out something of the position of the group members in relation to the proposed study. Taking time to find out what a given theme or unit means to those persons who are to be involved would be a very elementary step. Two specific questions might help:

1. *What do we already know about the proposed area of study?* (Answers to this might come by using such pro-cedures as discussion in small groups or the total group, by making drawings, by completing some metaphors that would be pertinent to the study, by seeing what some of the important words of the proposed theme might mean to the members, or by a short quiz.) No attempt is made to put anyone on the spot, but rather to find out what the cumulative thinking of the group might be.

Often a person who feels inferior and who may be lack-ing in knowledge will have the courage to ask some ques-tions if he hears someone he respects ask a question that may be similar to one he had. We are fearful of exposing our ignorance before our friends, and yet the very ques-tions that trouble us may trouble them. From such an informal session the alert leadership team or designated leader will pick up some cues as to the kind of knowledge the group needs.

2. *What do we want to find out?* As group members try to identify what they want to know, after having revealed some of what they don't know, they are ready to chart their course for learning. When any person discovers there is something he doesn't know but that he would like to know, he is usually motivated to the point that he will make an effort to learn. Unless he is willing to do this, his knowledge cannot increase. (Too often, group members take what the leader offers without realizing that these sessions could be meaningful learning times. They *could* gain knowledge, understanding, and skill that relate to real life problems and concerns.)

The pursuit of learning is enhanced when a person becomes aware of some things he does not know, is pointed to the resources that may assist him, and then moves in the direction of making the discoveries. This is the time when any learner may realize the joy of discovery and the thrill of learning something new. The desire must come from within the learner. Leadership teams and designated leaders may help—but the learner must *want* to learn.

The ultimate in lessening the deficiencies in knowledge within a group comes when each learner himself is aware of his need and commits himself to doing something about it. By the teaching design they establish, group leaders may make some of these discoveries; but the extent to which they will be able to effect change in the knowledge of another will be largely dependent upon the learner.

Sessions need to be fresh, filled with new ideas and, if not new knowledge, knowledge that can be used in new ways in the contemporary life of men.

Inventing Solutions

Several years ago a little puzzle was published in which the reader was asked to connect nine dots—three rows of three dots each, forming a square—by drawing four straight lines. The lines would go through all nine dots, but through each dot only once (without the pencil being lifted from the paper). Many struggled to do this but with no success, for they wanted to keep the lines within the box formation. In order to solve the problem the lines had to be extended beyond the bounds of the square.

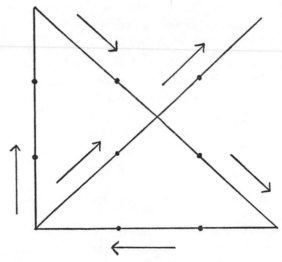

Perhaps many learning experiences have conditioned adults to stay within the box. In such a process the learner is kept from the joyous thrill of learning and of creating something with his very own ideas. How can we work creatively in seeking solutions to task and group situations?

A First Step

Irving R. Weschler identifies one of the characteristics of a creative person as sensitivity to surrroundings.[1] A simple exercise may point out to group members how little they actually observe:

• Place a number of objects (approximately twenty) on a table. Display them for a few seconds, then remove or cover the objects, and ask the group members to write down everything they saw.

• Use a number of sound-producing items from behind a screen, then ask the persons to identify the sounds. These should be fairly common sounds.

The day you propose to involve a group in working toward some creative solutions, ask them to do a trial run on a simple problem such as the following: How many uses can you make of a paper clip? Let them work for a couple of minutes, and then see how many ideas are given. They will recognize the need to think beyond the usual patterns.

Working for Solutions for Real Problems

The Family of Man,[2] created by Edward Steichen, contains an excellent selection of photographs about man. Groups might mount some of the pictures found on pages 144-53 or pictures gathered from other sources which portray loneliness, mercy and pity, calamity, and hunger. Give

[1] *The Leader and Creativity* (New York: Association Press, 1962), p. 15.

[2] *Family of Man* (New York: Simon & Schuster, 1956).

these pictures to conversation groups of two or three persons, and ask them to work through some solution of the problem being encountered—whether it is loneliness, death, war, poverty, old age, hunger. Another time you might use similar pictures from your own community.

Using the Element of Surprise

"Did you see that nice young couple dressed as hippies this morning?" Yes, it really happened in a local church where a group of young college students had decided they wanted to make a study of the hippies. On the opening day of the discussion their leaders came dressed as hippies (minus the long hair). An element of surprise? Yes. The group's curiosity and expectancy had been generated by this change in clothes.

A good procedure used constantly soon becomes ineffective. An element of surprise tends to keep a group on its toes and curiosity at a peak.

Audio Aids

An element of surprise can be inserted into a learning session in many ways. This may come at the very beginning of the session with, for example, a different room arrangement and pictures, placards, and magazines all about the room. (This would be most appropriate if consideration is being given to what people are reading and seeing today.) Another time the members may be greeted with blasts from many sources simultaneously—record player, television, tape recorder. (Some may say this is no different from home, but they may be surprised to encounter it at the church.)

Tape recordings can be used in many different and effective ways since they can be taped and checked for the desired effect before the session. Interrupting a discussion with a tape recording may startle a group and move them to thinking and feeling in a way that mere talk will not do.

Selections from recordings can be used very effectively at different times in a session. If the leader team has these aids located in an inconspicuous spot with a specific person operating them, the effect can be much sharper and more surprising, for the audience will not be wondering when they will be used.

Recordings of the two musicals by Helen Kromer, *For Heaven's Sake*[1] and *Sure as You're Born*,[2] have some choice pieces about relationships, communications, the smugness of the church, suburbia, the pulpit and the pew, and so forth. In a study of worship—or in the worship service itself—the record *Rejoice*[3] would offer a surprise element to those who have a narrow concept of worship.

The Unexpected Interruption

Persons in the audience may be coached to do certain things at an appointed time in order to get audience re-

[1] 33⅓ rpm recording, Christian Society for Drama, 120th and Broadway, New York, New York 10027.
[2] Available from Audio Visual Department, United Christian Missionary Society, 222 South Downey Street, Indianapolis, Indiana 46207.
[3] Scepter Records, 254 West 54th Street, New York, New York.

action and adaptation to a situation. For example, hecklers might be staged to make an appearance that could make the discussion more spontaneous.

Visual Aids

Anything that is a change from the usual procedure has the possibility of serving as a surprise or attention getter. Sometimes it may be as simple as displaying a large abstract drawing; colors that move in a somewhat psychedelic fashion; a blown-up cartoon; a projected picture from a filmstrip or opaque projector; tools such as saws, hammers, files, hoes; toys; sports equipment. (One group portrayed a young man coming to a weekend retreat loaded with golf clubs, fishing tackle box, tennis racket, diving equipment. He got attention, and quickly.)

An attention getter for a group that has had little involvement might be a sheet on which is printed a thought for them to discuss, paraphrase, or write a newspaper article about. A brief portrayal of a biblical situation, either in biblical or modern dress, could stimulate enthusiasm and might assist the group in seeing the contemporary quality of the Scriptures.

At another time members might present a courtroom scene in which the accused would have to make a defense of his position. (He might be charged with stirring up the people because he is seeking to get some action to improve some of the sore spots in the community.)

Any group has the possibility of using many exciting surprise elements. If they provide the opportunity, individuals can conceive and implement creative ways of making more realistic the intersection of the gospel with persistent life concerns.

Developing Listening Skills

Though persons spend a large portion of their time in listening to words and sounds, few have had any training or help in listening for meanings. One key to effective communication is the ability to listen to another and to hear the intent of his words—to get his message.

An audience can be helped to move from passive to active listening by identifying some listening tasks, whether the material to be heard is presented by a resource speaker, a tape, a record, or by one or several members of the group. Each team will be asked to listen for one specific idea or meaning. After the presentation the group will discuss what the different teams heard in response to their assigned listening tasks.

Listening groups provide immediate feedback to the speaker and to those responsible for the session. This means that clarification of obscure points can be made immediately and the dissemination of misinformation lessened. In some sessions, the listening groups will have opportunity to ask questions of either the resource person or those in charge of the meeting. When an entire audience is given some direction as to what to listen for, there can be almost 100 percent involvement of the group, though there may be only one person actually involved in the oral communication process. The structuring of an audience for active listening is such a simple process to set up that it could be used effectively much more often.

Listening Is Difficult

Though many sounds force their way into our hearing, persons have the strange ability to shut out those sounds and ideas they do not want to hear. This means that a particular message may be heard at one time and not another, depending upon the listener's need and attention.

Really hearing what another person is trying to say to us carries with it some risk, for becoming truly aware of the other's meaning may necessitate change on our part. Being "all there" when another is speaking is work, for it is an attempt to understand truly what the other is saying with his words and with his whole being. Sometimes the words are incidental, for the speaker may be in search of a listener—someone to hear him. For example, many youth and adults say, "Nobody listens to me." But we can develop the difficult but worthwhile art of listening.

Learning to Listen

Skill in listening to another person could be increased by using some of the ideas set forth on pages 65-68.

The less the listener assumes he has heard, and the more he works for feedback, the greater the accuracy of his listening should be. This calls for sensitivity to the speaker, to his world, and to his words. It is of major importance that the listener seek to understand the intent of the speaker's words.

Listening skills may be enhanced by a person serving in

the observer role. He might be acting with freedom to interrupt the group at any time when it appears they have not really heard what another was saying. The interruption might take a form like these: "What did you hear Jim saying?" "What was John trying to say to the group?" "How well are you listening to one another right now?" "What are we saying?" This kind of interruption can help a group look at itself immediately and make an assessment of its listening without a great loss of time.

A very simple listening exercise that could be used with any size group would be the formation of triads—groups of three persons. Each of the three would have a specific task. One person would be the teller (A), the second person (B) the listener, and the third person (C) the observer. The assignment would involve A telling something to B. B could only ask questions or restate. He would concentrate on listening, "attending" to the speaker. C would be the silent observer, taking note of ways in which B did not really hear A and making some observations regarding ways in which the listening might have been more accurate—always testing his perception at this point with A and B.

Concluding a Unit

A unit of adult study may seem to end, not with a bang, but with a whimper. People become a little tired of it; it does not seem to be producing the results that were hoped for. And in getting ready for the next unit, you as the leader are finding yourself distracted from the current study.

No meaningful study is ever finished, of course. But the lack of a sense of completion keeps many adult study groups in the doldrums. They just go on from meeting to meeting with no excitement of a new start and no satisfaction of a job well done. Here are some suggestions to help your group gain a sense of completion at the close of a unit.

• Review. Does anything bring more of a "blah" reaction than reviews? However, the answer is not to discard the review but rather to rethink the method by which the functions of review are performed. The use of the total learning group in this process is one way to avoid creating boredom.

For one unit of study, experiment with the use of newsprint instead of a chalkboard. Through your steering committee, select a recorder for the unit. When questions are raised, have him jot the question down on the newsprint. When discussion produces a series of possibilities or answers, have him record them with a brief notation. This will later remind those who were present of that high light, that insight, or that new idea.

Newsprint has the virtue of semipermanence. As the study develops, the sheets can be tacked or taped along a wall, giving a visual record of the group's life. This provides a continuous, week-by-week review.

• A scrapbook could be used. It may contain reference to the task forces in action, or clippings from the church bulletins or town newspaper which relate to the study. Some danger exists of this record becoming merely historical, so remember that this is not a memoir but a progress report.

• At the end of a unit, chart the flow of consequences of the study. (This, too, can be done on a piece of newsprint.) For instance, one group asks the members at the end of a unit to note the persons being affected by the study. The following chart shows some of the possible consequences.

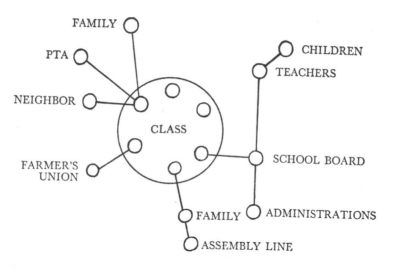

• Evaluation. This can be done at the end of a study, preferably under the direction of the steering committee. Through use of a simple questionnaire, get honest, anonymous reactions of members to the study. Not just "good" or "poor," but places at which it was helpful, how it was helpful, and so forth. This will guide both you and the steering committee as you plan for the future.

• Subjective evaluation. On the last day of a unit of

study bring paper, crayons, finger paints, marker pens, clay, or even old picture magazines, with scissors and glue. Ask each member to roll up his sleeves and go to work on "What this unit has meant to me." He is to draw a sketch, write a skit, model a sculpture, paste up a montage, or whatever else will give him a chance to express his impressions. Allow time at the close to talk about these expressions with one another.

• Report to the whole congregation. If genuine learning is going on, why keep it to yourselves? Most church bulletins and newsletters announce upcoming studies or speakers, and frequently that is the last anyone hears of them. Follow up your announcements with reports. Don't wait until the end; let others know that some exciting, useful learning is taking place.

Your classroom can present a report also. In a typical church when one walks into a children's classroom, it announces its learnings—on the tables or hanging on the walls. Walk into the typical adult classroom, and you see no sign of learning. It looks like a room to relax in, not to learn in. Change this—and when children come streaming into your room at the end of the hour to see what you have been doing, you'll know you are letting the church learn from your learnings.

Ways of Learning

Consultation

A *consultation* is any process whereby two or more persons together consider a given subject, question, or set of questions. This procedure can be scheduled months in advance, bringing together twenty to thirty persons experienced in the matter to be explored. Or it might involve as few as two persons discussing a problem on short notice. In other words, a consultation occurs when persons with important data on a specified problem provide adequate understanding of the matter.

A consultation can be helpful in a local learning group in several ways.

1. This way of learning can provide a reliable input of information on a subject.

2. A consultation provides opportunity to present opinions as well as factual information.

3. A consultation provides for statements that may represent each of several sides of the same problem as seen from different experiences. For example, a consultation on inner city slums might include a slumlord, a housing authority official, a health department representative, slum residents, and persons speaking for various groups working to change conditions in the area.

4. This method can draw experts to your group with ample time for you to learn their perspectives on the matter being considered.

5. A consultation also is an opportunity to consider problems and their possible solutions.

When Can a Consultation Be Used?

First, a consultation might be a way to launch the study of a particular study series. The topic might be related to a social issue, biblical scholarship, church history, or other subjects.

Second, a study of a particular topic may lead to the listing of important questions that still need investigation. A consultation can dig in on those questions. The questions become the focus for the consultation, and you may want to draw in some experts or put a few members to work as special consultants on specific questions. A consultation of this nature might be carried on as a regular part of your group work, or it might be set up as a special event.

A third situation that might call for a consultation involves the need for a particular type of information. You might arrange a taped interview with an authority on the topic and replay the tape for the group. You might arrange a long distance call and use an amplifier to bring the whole group in on the conversation.

A fourth idea for using the consultation method is to plan for an extended consultation. Here you will be thinking of at least several hours as a minimum, possibly a two-day meeting that might have several sessions. I would suggest this procedure for every study group at least once a year. It will bring vitality, direction, and cohesiveness as well as new information to your group.

Making Preparations for a Consultation

Whether you plan a ten-minute interview or a two-day consultation, there are some basic preparations to keep in mind:

1. State your basic question or problem in as clear a way as possible.

2. Develop a list of supplementary questions from the basic problem to be answered, so you will have some content for the whole consultation.

3. Be sure everyone participating, either as a group member or special consultant, has the basic question and the supplementary questions well in advance. Keep these questions before the group as you proceed, to avoid going off on tangents.

4. Take care in organizing. Designate the spots where you will need leadership. Plan the use of your time. Arrange for any special equipment, seat placement, and so forth.

A Legislative Hearing

A *hearing* is the process by which someone *listens* to the arguments and viewpoints intended to establish the nature of a problem and how it should be solved.

A *legislative hearing* is the process by which legislators, usually as a committee of the legislature, listen to arguments about a subject on their agenda. The viewpoints may be from individuals or from groups of citizens. The committee members listen in order to determine the extent and direction needed for enacting laws or changes in the law.

Two teaching/learning suggestions can be made here. You might use these procedures as given below or adapt them to your group's needs.

First, leaders of any church group should consider the values that lie in getting class members to attend hearings that are held in your community. These hearings, usually called by some unit of government such as the city council or the board of education or your state legislature, are key opportunities to gain broad perspectives about local problems.

Occasionally a local hearing may be conducted by one of the houses of the U.S. Congress or a federal commission or agency. Attending these events gives one firsthand knowledge of the basic processes of government as it attempts to involve "the people" in making decisions and determining directions for the future. And, almost every topic that might be discussed at such a hearing would involve a matter about which the responsible Christian citizen should hold an informed opinion.

In most hearings one discovers that Christians are often represented by more than one point of view. One Christian does not speak for all Christians. If we want our view to be heard, we must communicate it.

Most hearings are conducted in the evenings, especially if called by local agencies. Generally these deal with proposals for programs to solve some particular community or area problem such as housing, transportation, health services, welfare programs, education, zoning, or major changes in city charters, constitutions, or by-laws. The hearings are conducted because those who must make final decisions in behalf of all want to hear a cross section of the citizens' points of view. Afterward the persons conducting the hearing must recommend a solution to the problem and a way of getting it accomplished.

In the process of attending hearings we can become aware of our role as Christian citizens and responsible churchmen. If your group can attend a hearing, meet in advance to discuss the issue and plan to have one or more members of your group speak about the issue as they see it. Remember that one Christian does not necessarily speak for all Christian citizens.

A Moot Hearing

A second way to use a hearing as a learning method is to conduct a moot hearing (a let's-pretend one) within your own group. This procedure will be well suited to studies about the church's role in many of the social crises of our day. Matters such as those mentioned above are naturals. By using this method you can actually transform your group meeting into an arena where issues are openly discussed.

I suggest using two sessions for this procedure. The first session can be spent in getting some common basic information about the issue. The task could be to phrase the question for a hearing. Then the persons who will conduct the hearing should be selected. Consider inviting a local official involved in the problem to act as chairman of your hearing. (Your ideas might even influence his thinking and his action regarding the matter.) Set the scene well. Perhaps you could meet in a courtroom or a small auditorium; if not, then adapt your room to a special atmosphere for the meeting.

Assign several individuals to come prepared to speak to the question at hand. Some members might present viewpoints that are not likely to be held by others in your group. But encourage your group members to speak their own opinions and convictions. You might ask those who wish to speak to indicate this on a sign-up sheet.

Allow time after the hearing to draw some conclusions from the experience. Perhaps ten minutes could be used to indicate some suggestions as to what to do about the issue under study.

Finally, and quite important, is there anything some of your members want to do about the issues you have considered? If you have conducted a real hearing dealing with real ideas and reactions, some of your group members may want to express their concern toward this issue and take some appropriate action. If so, suggest they meet together at the close of the meeting and set a time to work further.

A Press Conference

This is a good involvement procedure for dealing with a controversial subject.

A press conference is called by one who has newsworthy

information. It is generally for the purpose of giving newsmen an announcement about some particular position, decision, problem, or action.

When you are considering the use of this method, give some serious thought to conducting a real press conference. Often a serious group of churchmen have significant statements to make which might be well received by the local press. Indicate to the press the particular kind of information you have and that you believe that it will be newsworthy.

If you are not successful in arranging a press conference, you can do the next best thing—plan to use the press-conference procedures in a class session. Assign roles to several members of your group as representatives of the several news media—television, radio, and press—local, national, and international.

After the announcement, most press conferences are turned into open question-and-answer sessions. Newsmen ask the questions and the announcing officer or his associates reply.

Steps in Preparation for a Press Conference:

1. Prepare the room for the conference. Use some props to give it the proper atmosphere, such as real microphones. Plan a formal setting. The news release announcers should be in a central location and visible to all participants.

2. Prepare a concise statement of the issue at hand. If you are making this the ending of a study of a particular topic, one whole session might be used by group members in working out the most significant element for the announcement. The supplementary elements that help clarify the main statement should be identified.

3. Assign roles to those who make the announcement, to those who will act as newsmen, to those who will answer the questions that follow. Group members who are to be newsmen might prepare some really sharp and pointed questions. The contents of their questions need not be disclosed until the proper time following the news announcement.

4. Have the announcement made orally and then distributed in mimeographed form to everyone. Questions can then refer directly to the statement.

5. Conduct the question-and-answer session.

6. After the conference divide your whole group into small working teams, giving each an assignment to prepare a news release based on the press conference. You might want to diversify the assignments with these types of categories:

• Newspaper, religious news section
• Newspaper, general news
• Magazine, editorial page

You can use the same categories for radio and television.

7. Plan the following week's meeting so that you can use the releases the groups will have prepared. A few props could create additional interest for the radio and television releases or reports.

8. Consider larger uses of your material. If you have used real material for the announcement and really serious and imaginative effort in putting together the releases and reports, you may have an item of interest. Perhaps now the local press will be interested and will help your announcement reach more people. Or see if the material is useful and of interest to the church or some groups in the church.

Making an Opinion Survey

Adults learn best what has relevance and importance for them.

Interest also has a great deal of effect on what a person chooses to do. But interest may be a static or an expanding factor. Adult education is seriously committed to the task of expanding our horizons to include new areas of interest. It is only as adults continue to learn that they are able to meet the demands of a changing world.

Research in adult education has revealed that answers for many problems faced by adults cannot be answered simply by "yes" or "no" and "right" or "wrong." Adults are faced with many situations in which one choice is no better than another except as the adult himself gathers facts about the situation, analyzes these facts, and then makes a choice.

If adults are highly motivated by their *interests* and by *securing facts for decision-making,* then educators and leaders of adults should consider the use of the *opinion survey* as one source of facts. That is, though a person's opinion is not a fact, it is a fact that he *has* an opinion.

Informal opinion surveys may be used regularly in our classes or groups to secure the views of individuals on a subject under discussion. If a class is to study a series of lessons on world peace, for example, it would be helpful for the leaders to prepare an instrument that would test the group's opinions on such subjects as the United Nations, Red China, Vietnam, and the Peace Corps. Greater honesty and less hesitancy in responding can be achieved if the answers remain unsigned.

Constructing an Effective Opinion Survey

1. The number of persons being surveyed and the procedures used in tabulating the results are important. In a local organization such as the church the number of people to be surveyed, the means of tabulating the results, and the statement of the questions are important factors if the results are to be understood and are to reflect any significant consensus.

2. The individual questions in a survey should be clear and contain only one major idea. Questions may be asked in such a way that they are answered by Yes or No. Other questions may be multiple choice, suggesting that the individual check or underline his answer. Still other questions can be designed that call for a brief comment or response. This procedure that provides for an open-ended response is the most difficult to tabulate, but it can be the most helpful in securing the actual thoughts of persons.

Many surveys of opinion are constructed as "intensity" scales. A statement is made such as, "It is good that Red China was admitted to the United Nations" or "Our church needs to reexamine its program with youth." The individual responds to the question on a five-point scale that ranges from *strongly agree* to *strongly disagree*. If the individual should check the middle position, for example, he would be considered neutral on the subject.

3. In conducting an opinion survey not only the questions but the instructions must be clear.

4. The design for an opinion survey should be consistent throughout the survey instrument. Jumping from one topic to another in the survey should be avoided as it may confuse the reader and negatively affect his answers.

5. Lastly, an opinion survey should be shared with and reported to the group that was surveyed. Persons are interested in the opinions of others and whether they themselves reflect majority or minority points of view. Also, as learners together, adults should be sensitive to the opinions of the group as a means of creating a better atmosphere for mutual conversation and discussion.

Opinions are the lifeblood of the learning process. They represent both our successes and failures in grappling with the issues we face. Through securing the opinions of its members a group can see where its members stand and begin to set new and helpful goals for itself.

Conducting a Colloquy

The colloquy is a group presentation procedure that is often used to overcome the lack of knowledge or skill on the part of the larger audience. Many times, however, extremely skilled and knowledgeable groups will use a colloquy to help sharpen the issues in a meeting or to overcome the disadvantages created by a large group, which makes general discussion difficult.

Basically, a colloquy is composed of selected members of a group who have been assigned to talk with one or more resource persons by asking questions and raising issues important to the audience. A moderator may preside and open the discussion for comment and question.

Often a colloquy meets with greater success than an open forum because the participants are chosen with thought to their interest and skill. The questions raised by the panel often are carefully phrased and seek to get to the heart of the issues being discussed. There is also less chance of diverging from the subject with such careful questioning. However, it can be safely assumed that a successful colloquy does not happen by chance; planning and preparation must be a part of its development.

A colloquy can also be conducted in situations with outside resource persons as participants. Thought should be given to the exact function that the resource people are to perform. Once basic decisions about the format have been made, a few members of the group can be selected to represent the other members and to question the resource people about issues that concern the group. Preplanning is helpful in shaping the questions and avoiding the repetition of ideas.

Here are two examples of possible settings in which a colloquy can be used:

1. A local church has retained an architect in preparation for a building program. The architect has worked with various committees in the church, including the education and worship commissions for the purpose of gathering the information needed for preliminary drawings. From the community he has gathered facts also about expected population increase and the nature of the real estate and labor markets. The building committee of the local church has worked closely with the architect and is completely familiar with his findings and drawings. The decision is made to present the information to the members of the congregation in order to secure their support and enthusiasm for the proposed program.

To make the presentation effective the architect will talk to the congregation about his findings and exhibit the preliminary drawings. Following the architect's statement, three members of the building committee will question the architect on issues that remain unclear. The questioners will seek to reflect issues that are problems in the minds of the members of the audience. After the inquiry by the members of the building committee, the audience is invited to ask any further questions.

2. Another group has been concerned about the increased interest in the so-called "new morality." Most of the class members are well-read parents who are confronted daily with decisions about how much freedom to give their teen-agers. After some discussion about how to proceed on this subject, a decision has been made to invite a high school principal and a juvenile court officer to the class session. Four class members have been instructed to question the resource people about their attitudes toward a curfew for youth, teen-age marriages, and what constitutes a healthy discipline for adolescents. Following the question period by the selected members, the juvenile specialists will be questioned by the entire class.

Conducting a colloquy can offer a *focused* learning experience for a group. It can uncover details about a subject which may be missed by the average class member. But conducting a colloquy can also be an experience in planning, the rudiments of which all adult groups need.

Diagraming

Diagrams are two-dimensional drawings. They may be outlines, sketches, simple maps, graphs, or symbols. They are not fine art, and no artistic skill is required to create teaching diagrams. They are visualizations of relationships, forces, quantities, spaces, magnitudes, directions, journeys, and so forth. They may demonstrate relationships, represent objects or areas, illustrate and compare forces, show quantities, explain values, and so on. They sometimes rely on color.

Here are descriptions of some uses diagrams may have in the teaching/learning process:

• Diagrams may be used to visualize the relationships between persons. Two familiar examples of this type of diagram are the family tree and the organizational chart. The family tree shows how a group of people are related by blood, and the organizational chart shows how people filling offices within an organization are related in function and authority.

• Diagrams may visualize the relationships between groups as well as between persons. Suppose a class wishes to act to influence policy on public housing in the community. Several groups in the local municipal government, as well as certain federal agencies, have a voice in the decision-making. A diagram that analyzes these groups, their relationships, and their relative importance, may help the class decide where to exert influence most strategically. The diagram on page 61 is an example of this use.

• Diagrams or charts may be helpful in analyzing strengths and weaknesses in procedures and relationships.

• Diagrams may summarize the historical development of movements, nations, or churches. The familiar "family tree of Protestant churches" is such a diagram. However, the usefulness of the diagram as an illustration of historical growth and change could be applied in other cases also.

Diagram the historical development of your local church. Use a diagram in learning about the history of church architecture. Show in a diagram the historical development of hymnody, indicating the key persons in the development. An excellent example of a diagram used to show the historical development of musical instruments is in Volume 13 of *The World Book Encyclopedia.*

• Diagrams may be used to visualize sequence. Very often a class needs help in understanding clearly the sequence of steps that is required for the execution of a plan. A class may have a goal that needs to be achieved in stages. At the same time there may be confusion in the class about the sequence the steps must follow if the goal is to be reached. A diagram can often clarify such confusion. For example, a class may decide to increase the power of its voice in the official councils of the local church. They may decide to do this in stages over a period of two years. The sequence of these stages may be essential to the strategy. A diagram may help as the strategy develops.

• A diagram may be used to aid in the identification of objects or to distinguish very small differences between similar objects. For example, Christians who are learning to identify Christian symbols need diagrams to help them learn this skill. When a symbol exists in a variety of closely related forms, as, for example, the cross does, diagrams can help the student identify and recognize these varieties of one symbol.

• Diagrams may be used to take notes on visual observations. The biology student in the laboratory records in a diagram what he sees beneath the microscope. A faithful member in your church school class may be asked to help evaluate your class. He may be asked to notice who speaks to whom in class discussions, and to notice over a period of weeks how and where class members choose to sit as they arrive. Such observations can be recorded and reported in diagrams, called sociograms. They may help a team of leaders from the class evaluate the life of the class and plan how to increase involvement.

You could easily find many more uses for diagrams. The above suggestions may stimulate your imagination. You might use two other sources: turn through *The World Book Encyclopedia,* look at each diagram, and think of similar ways they could be used in your adult class. Also look through *Thinking With a Pencil,* by Henning Nelms.[1]

Audience Reaction Teams

An audience reaction team is a real asset to the learning situation when a resource person is to be present. There is usually some concern that he may speak too technically or in a jargon that is unfamiliar to the majority of those present.

Purpose of the Team

The members of the audience reaction team would seek to hear the resource speaker through the ears of the

[1] (New York: Barnes & Noble, 1964.)

larger audience—hearing how it must be sounding to them. At any point when the reaction team feels that the speaker is no longer communicating because of his use of words, ideas, or concepts, they interrupt and ask questions of him. The team might be asking for more illustrations, for definitions, for clarification. The team seeks to facilitate communication between the speaker and the audience by not permitting the speaker to continue to use words that are not being understood. For the best work, the team needs to know the audience quite well or have the ability to identify closely with it. They would also be a more effective team if they had some understanding of the topic under discussion.

Composition of the Team

The reaction team most appropriately would be made up of persons representing different points of view. For example, you might be having a presentation on "The Church in Mission in Our Community" and the speaker is someone affiliated with the community council. It would be good to have a woman, a man, a youth, and perhaps a retired person on the reaction team, for the needs of the community and the approach that might be made to these needs might be viewed differently by persons of different sexes and different generations.

Functions of the Team

The first and foremost function of the team has already been given—namely, to facilitate communication and keep the speaker from losing the audience.

Second, a very important concurrent learning would be that the reaction team may be giving support and help to other members of the audience as they formulate questions. In addition, because of this support some persons might be willing to serve as members of the team at a later time.

Once the reaction team has assisted in opening up the subject at the audience level, a great deal of audience participation may follow the dialogue.

Value of the Team

Many times groups have had a team of persons who have responded to a whole presentation by a speaker, but sometimes in doing this they have been reacting to a speech and not seeking to assist the communication process between the speaker and the audience.

The use of more audience reaction teams would do much to improve communication. We use many resource persons from our communities without getting their message across. How helpful it would be to have three to five persons take the role of the questioner and seek to keep the channels of communication flowing!

Sometimes the audience reaction member may say, "Is this what you are saying?" or "Is this another way of saying it?" He would be putting the technical language into popular phraseology. An alert, keen audience reaction team can do much to keep the speaker and the audience on their toes. The ability and willingness of the audience to listen and to understand and thus be involved should be furthered by the use of an audience reaction team.

When to Use an Audience Reaction Team

A team can be used effectively when you know the speaker is likely to use technical language that will not be understood by the majority of the listeners. With a group that has been accustomed to just sitting and listening, the audience reaction team may provide a breakthrough for more active involvement of all members.

In a group that is moving from dependency upon the leader to dependency upon the group, the audience reaction team may provide an intermediary step.

In an era of knowledge explosion and specialization more audience reaction teams are needed to aid the average audience of laymen in understanding the words and meaning of specialists.

Using Rhythmic Movement

In one particular scene from *Zorba the Greek*, Zorba expresses his feelings like this:

Whenever I feel I'm choking with some emotion, [something inside me says] Dance! and I dance, and I feel better. [Men have] let their bodies become mute and they only speak with their mouths. But what d'you expect a mouth to say? What can it tell you? If only you could have seen how [my friend] listened to me from head to foot, and how he followed everything. I danced my misfortunes; my travels; . . . the trades I'd learned, how I'd been shoved into prison. [He] could understand everything. My feet and my hands spoke, so did my hair and my clothes. When I finished, [he] hugged me in his arms, . . . [and] we wept and laughed in each other's arms.[1]

This scene has something to say to the whole realm of Christian education. The church is called to be a community that participates in the communication and celebration of the gospel. This scene, more specifically, points out the value of rhythmic movement in communication and celebration. (One is reminded of the experience of David [II Samuel 6:16-22].)

We in the twentieth century are bombarded with words —television, newspapers, volumes of written materials. Zorba was right when he said that men have allowed their bodies to become mute.

How right we are when we emphasize the soul and speak of the feelings of man! Yet, the body is a part of man's total self. The body is the only means by which man can communicate, and thus it is the only means by which he can hear the Word of God.

The Christian faith does not speak merely of man's religious self. The Christian faith speaks to the whole man— to his mind, his emotions, and his body. Our task is to help man understand himself, his human situation, and to respond in love to God and neighbor. Further, our task is to allow man to express his whole self in freedom.

The role of rhythmic movement in Christian education is to allow man to express freely all that he is. This can best be done as the whole man participates in the act of communication. How do we begin? First by relaxing. With the help of music we can use our arms and feet to express

[1] Nikos Kazantzakis, *Zorba the Greek* (New York: Simon & Schuster, 1959), pp. 85-87.

what the music says to us. We can let that which is within us come out as we listen to the music. Having allowed our voices to do all our communicating, we will find it difficult to come out with our whole selves.

In one adult experience a group member took a piece of tissue paper and wadded it up. The other group members were to act as that paper, using their bodies. Then the paper was unwadded, and the group continued to act like the paper, then like a piece of bent wire, a limp ribbon, a piece of glimmering tinsel, and other similar objects. Second, the group was asked to express hate and loneliness at the same time. Other emotions followed: fear, happiness, anger, hostility, love, joy, thankfulness. Unable to use the voice in any way, the group had to rely solely on the body. The group gradually gained its freedom to move and express.

We celebrate the gift of grace as we study, worship, and serve in the world. Just as man needs to communicate with all that he is, so he needs to celebrate with his wholeness. Rejoice and dance, for he is risen.

Using Choral Reading

One of the distinctive aspects of the Christian faith in contrast to religions outside the Christian tradition is its communal character. The Christian is truly Christian only as he lives out his life in community, in "common" with other Christians. This characteristic of being "in common" or in community is an essential part of that Word which is proclaimed in preaching and in the sacraments.

Choral reading can be a living symbol of the "community of proclaimers." Too often members of this community of proclaimers become individual observers, having no share in the proclaiming or the proclaimed. Choral reading can be a means by which persons share in the proclaiming and in that which is proclaimed, a means whereby the student participates in the teaching/learning process. As persons participate as one in communion, they also can participate as one in proclamation.

These points can be illustrated by looking at ways of using choral reading in study groups. A young adult group may be studying current political or social issues. Let us assume that the issue is poverty. An interesting way to use choral reading would be to take verses from Isaiah 1, emphasizing the lines that refer to injustice. With proper voice inflection and mood, parts of this chapter could be presented with moving power.

Another way of dealing with this same issue is to ask members of the group to devise a litany for use in the group. Still another way would be to ask for poetic expressions that could be used as choral readings.

Using biblical texts in dramatic ways helps persons become personally and open-mindedly involved in the biblical drama itself. The story of the Samaritan woman at the well is a moving story, and if presented in dramatic ways it can move people in today's world. The biblical resources for acting out the faith are almost unlimited. Choral reading can be a means whereby a group can participate in the acting, as is done when persons act out the faith in Baptism and Holy Communion.

Many writers are now combining choral reading with individual dialogue in plays for churches. Phillip Turner's

Christin in the Concrete City[1] can be presented as a choral reading. This technique can serve as a discussion starter when a group is willing to take a biblical text and present it in such dramatic fashion.

In preparing a biblical text for choral reading a group needs to decide on the key words in the text, where accents should be, where phrases should be said with strength, and where they should be said with restraint. Each person might have somewhat different feelings about the places to use the inflections, as different words will have different meanings for each person.

The actual class discussion of where emphasis should be placed is of tremendous value in the preparation. This discussion will not only serve as a basis for the treatment of some passage; it will also give the group members a chance to hear, analyze, and become enriched by several interpretations of the passage. In preparing Psalm 23 for a choral reading, some might stress "Lord," and others "my," and still others "shepherd" in verse 1. As group members share the reasons certain words have more meaning than others for them and why they feel certain words should be stated emphatically, the total group comes to learn more about the group members—their feelings, attitudes, and convictions.

By working through to some common understanding of the Scripture (or whatever material is used), group members will learn more about the faith and what it really means to be a "community of faith."

Harmony is an important factor in choral reading. This

---

[1] In John W. Bachman and E. Martin Brown, *Better Plays for Today's Churches* (New York: Association Press, 1964).

does not mean that every group member will agree on the meaning of a passage. It does mean, however, that group members are able to share their differences, allowing freedom of expression, and in the light of their differences develop harmonious reading. The harmony comes as group members allow one another to express themselves freely, and it then culminates in the group reading together.

Choral reading can be a fairly simple means of getting a number of persons involved in dramatic presentations of the faith. Persons can grow in their faith as they become a part of the church's ministry of proclamation.

Learning Through Social Pressure

In recent years in America we have seen a reversal of the traditional roles in the teaching/learning process. We have discovered that the young have become the teachers and the old the learners about many issues. How has this come about?

We have a generation of young men and women who have forced the older generation and its establishment to examine their doings in areas of race, human rights, war, peace, the draft, higher education, job training, and the relationship of law to justice. This reversal has been accomplished almost solely with one method: social pressure. The classroom has been the public arena; the interpreters have been the news media; and the intent has been to put pressure on the ultimately responsible citizen so that he has had to rethink issues he has previously accepted without question.

If teaching and learning are measured by the degree of behavioral change they bring about, then this method of social pressure must be recognized as a highly effective teaching/learning method.

The problem we face with this method is that it intentionally creates a conflict situation. Most persons in the church have the idea that all conflict, hostility, or tension is a sign of either evil or weakness; but this is not necessarily the case.

Social pressure has a very strong relationship to Christian teaching and tradition.

Premises

The first premise in the social pressure method is that there are social injustices that have been accepted or tolerated too long. As Christians we should recall that the first premise of the Scriptures is the recognition and reminder that all men, including ourselves, are evil; none is perfect.

The second premise of social pressure is that we have the ability and also the responsibility humanely to expose wrong wherever it exists. Our Christian tradition clearly teaches us that to be obedient to the witness of Jesus is openly to recognize and assume personal responsibility for what is evil.

The third premise of social pressure is that when injustice exists something can be done about it. The thesis is that man is responsible for building a better world in which to live. No view of Christian discipleship would be adequate without the declaration that with the help and guidance of the Spirit men can continue to "overcome evil with good."

The fourth premise of social pressure is that the source of the evil or wrong must be identified. One remembers Jesus naming the Pharisees and the moneychangers as people who led the Jewish nation in wrong directions. Wrong or evil practices exist only because someone is perpetuating them. Jesus knew this, and those who use social pressure effectively also know it.

Social pressure proceeds on the fifth premise that right will triumph over wrong, that justice will be victorious over injustice.

Dangers

Certain dangers are present in the use of this method. The greatest is that it pits the power of one view of how life should be lived against another idea of how life should be lived.

Related dangers are inherent in the difficulty of deciding which is the right concept of how life should be lived. The Christian understanding champions the rights of the minority.

Another danger is that victory can bring a sense of power over the loser. This sense of power can result in the person's using social pressure for private or personal ends rather than to right wrongs.

The goal of any effort to use social pressure in teaching/learning is to bring enough threats of insecurity to a given group of people that they will begin to re-evaluate their own ideas and beliefs about the issue put before them.

Purposes

The civil rights movement of the mid-sixties was a most effective effort in social pressure. It was carried out primarily by a Christian group, the Southern Christian Leadership Conference, and led by a minister, Martin Luther King, Jr. The reason for some of the "extreme" demonstrations, as some called them, can only be understood when one realizes that the whole movement was designed as an attempt to get the nation as a whole to take a look at what the demonstrators believed were wrongs and injustices in the society.

Wherever demonstrations were conducted, people discussed their views not only about demonstrations but about the more basic issues—the place and rights of the black people in America. They taught America something we had put off facing for more than a hundred years.

When a small group of church members chooses to use this tool, you may find that a whole congregation will begin to change its attitudes and ways of thinking.

Using Business Management Techniques

Some of the most exciting adult education is going on in business circles. Many companies are putting considerable money into educational leadership and are allowing these leaders freedom to experiment.

A department store in Pittsburgh employed a well-qualified educator and assigned him the task of providing training for every member of the staff. He went about it on an individual basis. After getting the necessary background information about each of the employees, he met with them individually and worked out annually a personalized plan of study and growth. Only after he had progressed in planning individualized study designs did he set up any classes and other types of group meetings. He set these up only at the points where the personalized programs for several persons overlapped. This educator did not hesitate to set up a course for only two or three people or to provide a learning opportunity for one person.

Time Blocks

A large computer company has a top trainer who makes use of concentrated learning in two- and three-week blocks of time. Groups of employees in multiples of twelve are housed on a college campus or in a motel away from home where he can get their full attention. He uses twelve as his basic grouping, for it can be subdivided in several ways for different tasks: two groups of six, three groups of four, four groups of three, or six groups of two. He makes considerable use of these different sub-groups. Each learner is a member of a specific group of twelve and gets to know these persons well. When he meets in smaller groups, the membership is from this group of twelve.

In these several weeks of concentrated study this trainer makes use of carefully selected readings and gives a set of books to each student. When a student arrives at the site of the conference, the books are in his dormitory room, and he is the only one in this room.

Sensitivity

Sensitivity training is a part of these conferences, as it is of many other business community efforts to help employees grow in effectiveness, both as employees and as persons. Such training is designed to help persons become more aware of their part in face-to-face relations and to increase their ability to communicate and relate to others on a meaningful level.

The important interdependence of communication and face-to-face relationships can no longer be ignored. As Harold J. Leavitt points out in his book *Managerial Psychology,* "Communication is a basic tool of relationships. In most relationships it is simultaneously a tool for information gathering and for influence by *all* members of the relationship.

"People begin, modify, and end relationships by communicating with one another. Communication is their channel of influence, their mechanism of change." [1]

Case Study

Case study is another method the computer company trainer uses to advantage. In preparation for these conferences he spends considerable time and energy writing up several specific problem cases, putting in the data that are needed to analyze the situation and to work toward

[1] (Chicago: The University of Chicago Press, 1964) , pp. 137-38.

possible solutions. In the conference, after the students become familiar with the details of the case, they are given parts and role-play the situation. They look for a solution not only on the intellectual and academic level but also on the feeling level.

A variety of settings and methods is characteristic of much education in business circles. We have already mentioned the method of problem-solving through role-playing (spontaneous acting out of solutions). Other business training methods that are in vogue are, according to Leavitt, job rotation, an up-through-the-ranks form of training; classroom training; apprenticeship systems; and the "junior management board," a provisional group that allows the trainee to be "manager for a day," learning as he acts as a manager. Business has a wide variety of training techniques, and a similar variety is being emphasized in the church.

Those who serve as consultants in local churches often observe that persons who resist innovation in church adult education are excited about the interesting learning opportunities in which they are involved in their vocational fields. When they see that the settings and methods that are so valuable in their profession are applicable to the church, they get excited about the possibilities there. It is hoped that they will remain interested enough to bring these methods into use in the church's adult study.

The congregation of nearly every church has persons who are in training programs connected with their employment. Wise leaders of adults can seek out these persons, inquire about their training programs, and encourage them to help devise settings and procedures that can forward the educational purposes of the church.

Using Paints

One alternative to parrot learning (giving back the same words or ideas received without knowing their meaning) is to have the learner translate the ideas from one medium to another. Paints can help. If the idea was received through the medium of spoken or written words, the task can be to present it in a painted image or symbol.

Interpretation

Here is one illustration of the use of paints.

A certain study group was working on the concept of "ministry." They had read several of the current treatments of the subject and had listed the elements that make up local church ministry in our present day. Their discussion had become heavy with words, with more intellectual content than feeling. Someone suggested that they try to express how their ideas felt to them. This led to work with tempera paints and two-by-three-foot sheets of paper. With the list of elements in mind, and their reading and discussion behind them, they attempted to express their feelings with paint on paper.

A committee of three put a church building modeled after their own in the center of a table and circled it with a series of small pictures depicting acts of service and witness. They connected the church to the pictures with three-strand cords. The bright colors used gave a feeling of excitement and busyness.

Another person, who worked alone in depicting his idea of ministry, splashed a paper with colors and worked them into a series of concentric circles. Because his blues and greens suggested water, many viewers at first glance thought of a pebble dropped into a pond with ripples going out from it. But as they looked, the ripples also seemed to return toward the center.

In all the paintings, the colors and forms enabled class members to express feelings that were not easily communicated through words. As they compared their artistic descriptions, similarities of interpretation were noticed. This added an important dimension to their discussion.

Summary

Painting can also be used effectively to tie the sessions of a unit together and to provide the basis for summary. One class posted a five-by-eight-foot sheet of wrapping paper on a wall of their room and placed a set of assorted color felt markers nearby. During or after each session class members were free to paint a representation of an idea or a meaning that came from the discussion during the session. In some sessions several persons made their contributions to the mural. By the end of the study nearly everyone in the group had participated in this composite record. No attention was given to sequence or organization.

The result was an accumulation of images, forms, and colors that provided a configuration for many of the separate ideas that had emerged. Seeing them together in this unplanned way stimulated thinking about their interrelatedness. Thus a deeper unity was found in their study than that which came through in the logical organization and sequence of the sessions. In the final session an attempt to select a title for their cooperative work of art helped them summarize and evaluate their study experience.

Expression

Both finger painting and brush painting were put to good use in one weekend retreat. The finger painting was used at the beginning and the brush painting near the end. Bowls of finger paint were prepared, using laundry starch and tempera color with some talcum powder added for smoothness. After each person got settled in his cabin, he was encouraged to experiment with the finger paint on sheets of glossy shelf paper. Each was urged to express how he felt about the retreat. At the beginning of the first discussion period each person posted one of his creations. No attempt was made at this time to discuss or interpret the paintings.

Toward the end of the retreat, tempera paints and brushes were available, and each person was encouraged to use them to express some of the meaning the retreat had for him. This product was put beside the same person's finger painting, and in the final session each was asked to look at his own productions and share any thoughts he wished while he compared how he felt when he arrived with his feelings as the retreat closed.

The most valuable result was that each participant had several reminders of the retreat and its study emphasis. These were more significant than some hastily recorded notes on the study theme.

We have seen how paints can be used to express concepts of words in different media. They give each learner a means of individual expression. Painting can also be used to summarize a series of discussions, ideas, and experiences. Individually prepared pictures can be assembled into a larger, overall mural or configuration. An important idea to remember is the appropriate timing in the use of paints in adult study.

Planning a Festival of the Arts

An art festival is a time set aside in the life of a congregation to allow members to focus their whole attention on the beauty, insight, joy, and revelation that art can offer the Christian.

A group planning an art festival for a church needs to know what art may do. Art can be only illustration, helping people think visually about people and places. Art can be propaganda, as happens when the art form is used chiefly to push an idea. Art may be revelation, as when the art form unveils the mystery of God's presence. Art may be celebration, as when the art form allows the artist and the viewer to dance and rejoice in the presence of life. Art may be a stimulus to self-awareness, as when the art form leads the viewer to gaze within.

Art may serve to make some part of reality more vivid, as when a man turns from a painting of the sea to view the sea itself and discovers that the real sea is more vividly present because of the painting. Art may calm the soul with the presence of beauty, wholeness, harmony, and symmetry. Art may lead the viewer to see colors, forms, related masses, contrasts, symmetries, harmonies, and subtleties of hue and position for the first time.

In all these functions art gives life to man's spirit. In each of these functions art is related to some of the methods and the goals of Christian education.

The first step in planning an art festival may be a period of study by the planning committee. The committee may wish to clarify for itself the ways in which art may serve spirit. The role of beauty in the nurture of the spiritual life should be clear in the thought of the planning committee. Two helpful books that could be studied at this planning stage are *Sight and Insight,* by Richard Guggenheimer[1] and *A Theological Approach to Art,* by Roger Hazelton.[2] If several adult classes study such books at this planning stage, the congregation's preparation will be even better.

The planning committee is likely to wonder next about resources. Where can a church obtain art for exhibit and study? These are some avenues for exploration:

Many university art departments own collections of art. The great universities often own major collections, but almost every university with a significant art department has a small collection of its own. These paintings are often shared with local churches. Or the university may be willing to arrange a special exhibition in its own gallery which is suited to the purposes of your church's art festival. A university is more likely to do this if the festival is spon-

---

[1] (Port Washington, N.Y.: Kennikat Press, 1968.)

[2] (Nashville: Abingdon Press, 1967.)

sored by several churches or a metropolitan council of churches.

Your committee should contact local and regional artists. You can find guilds and leagues of artists in most cities and most regions. State governments sometimes have commissions of fine art. These commissions will know of local artists, and local art dealers and galleries will also. These artists will almost always cooperate with you in planning a festival. They want their work to be seen, enjoyed, and, of course, to be purchased. If you live in a big city, the Sunday edition of your newspaper may list several art displays that could also appear in your local church facilities.

Local and regional art museums will help you gather art for display in your church. Some museums have special collections they regularly circulate to schools and churches. Others have sales and rental galleries. Some sell reproductions, inexpensive prints, laminated plaques, framed reproductions, color slides, books about their own collections, manuals about special exhibitions, books on the theory and practice of art, and so forth. Some also have film libraries with resources about art on 16mm film.

Even museums that are not near you can help you if you write to them and in your letter provide a clear description of your needs. In particular you may find help from The National Gallery of Art, Constitution Avenue at Sixth Avenue, Northwest, Washington D.C. 20037. Write them and request a list of their publications, filmstrips, circulating slide sets, reproductions for sale, circulating exhibits, and so forth.

Do not overlook the help state governmental organizations can give. Some states have state art museums that offer several circulating exhibits of paintings, sculpture, and so forth. Investigate extension services in your state.

Finally, do not overlook the mechanics of displaying art. Refer to *Display and Exhibit Handbook,* by William Hayett.[3]

---

[3] (New York: Reinhold Publishing Corporation, 1967.)

Resources for Learning

Creeds

"Theology is inescapable in the educational enterprise. It can be ignored, with confusion as the inevitable consequence, but it cannot be eliminated as a factor in any educational situation." [1] This statement by James D. Smart, an outstanding Christian educator, suggests something of the importance of the theological dimension of our teaching ministry. Education in the church is education in the Christian faith and must therefore be concerned for both the cognitive and the experiential dimension of that faith. Because creeds deal with the historic statements—the cognitive aspect—of the faith of the church, they are an important factor in the church's educational ministry.

What will be our attitude toward creeds? What is their proper function in the life of the church? Are creeds to be considered the final word on the doctrines of the church? Do you agree with the statement in the preface to

[1] James D. Smart, *The Creed in Christian Teaching* (Philadelphia: The Westminster Press, 1962), p. 9.

119

"The Confession of 1967" of the United Presbyterian Church? It states, "Confessions and declarations are subordinate standards in the church, subject to the authority of the Scriptures which bear witness to Jesus Christ, the Word of God Incarnate. No one type of confession is exclusively valid, no one statement irreformable. Obedience to Jesus Christ alone identifies the one universal church and supplies the continuity of its tradition." [2]

Creeds are "working documents" that need to be used in Christian education. They seek to deal with the central issues of Christianity. Your attention is directed toward the "Korean Creed" of The United Methodist Church and "The Confession of 1967" of The United Presbyterian Church. Both these creeds are twentieth-century statements of the church.

Subjects for Study

What are some ways to use these and other creeds as subjects for study?

You could provide ample material for several sessions of discussion in depth by treating the theological content of any given creedal statement. Why not compare the Korean Creed to the Confession of 1967? At what points are they similar? How do these two twentieth-century creeds compare with the Apostles' Creed? Why is the Apostles' Creed so preoccupied with Jesus Christ?

You could use a creed as the basis for a systematic study of the historic doctrines of the faith. The book quoted above, *The Creed in Christian Teaching*, is an analysis of

[2] *The Proposed Book of Confessions* (United Presbyterian Church, 1966), p. 177.

the Apostles' Creed. It would be helpful to any group seeking to make a serious study of creedal statements.

Why not devise your own outline of study, using the Korean Creed? This creed was developed for use by the Methodists of Korea and is being used quite widely in Methodist churches.

Methods of Teaching

What are some methods for using creeds in teaching?

1. *Try your hand at paraphrasing or rewriting the creed.* One of the most helpful exercises for an adult learner who is seeking to appropriate personal meanings is to attempt to put into his own words what something means to him. A creedal statement could really come to life in this way.

Another dimension to paraphrasing is the help one receives in saying what he really means. Many thoughtful laymen have real difficulty with parts of the Apostles' Creed. This difficulty is illustrated in Leslie Weatherhead's *The Christian Agnostic*. With reference to the statement, "I believe in the resurrection of the body," Dr. Weatherhead suggests that we really mean, "I believe in the survival of personality," and we ought to say so.[3]

2. *Role play a group of churchmen attempting to formulate a statement of their faith.* It would be an interesting exercise for the participants as well as for the observers.

3. *Discover the biblical basis for the creed.* Ask members to take certain creedal statements and with the aid of a concordance, trace several passages of Scripture which

---

[3] (Nashville: Abingdon Press, 1965), p. 17.

deal with the subject. How well does the creed reflect the meaning of these related passages?

Creeds are useful tools in helping adults focus on the central issues of Christian faith. The leader of adult study groups should be aware of the help available from the various creedal statements of the church.

Cartoons

Cartoons can present life issues, including controversial subjects, in such a concrete, straightforward way that it is hard to bypass the issue at hand. The cartoonist often uses symbols to represent minority groups, nations, evils of our day, personalities in the news, and so on. These symbols are his means of expressing what another might say—or be unwilling to say—in an editorial article.

Too often church school classes discuss faith in "religious" language or clichés that avoid confronting the real issues of daily life. Cartoons offer the possibility of focusing on problems of family relationships, marital problems, race relations, and political issues in a disarming manner. Through the use of cartoons to start and focus a discussion, adults may more freely express their views on a particular subject as well as of life in general.

In a very concrete, humorous way a cartoon is able to pinpoint a whole style or philosophy of life. Such a cartoon is found in a small, stimulating book on theology: *The Gospel According to Peanuts,* by Robert L. Short.[1] (You might secure this book as a continuing teaching resource, for its many cartoon interpretations.)

[1] (Richmond: John Knox Press, 1965), p. 84.

In this cartoon strip, Lucy, the cantankerous little girl whose life mission seems to be to torment others, is sitting down discouraged, her head in her hands. Linus tries to console her by suggesting that life has its "ups and downs." But she can't understand why *her* life has to have its "ups and downs"—why she can't just move from one "up" to another "up" to an "upper up"? She finally shouts that she doesn't want *any* "downs"! She just wants "ups" and "ups" and "ups"! To this, Linus reacts in despair: he can't stand it.

If you can obtain a copy of the book, you might cut out this cartoon and mount it on an eight-by-ten-inch piece of cardboard and pass it around for each class member to view. Or an opaque projector could be used to show the cartoon on a screen.

The class might divide into groups if there are enough copies of the cartoon. Different questions might be asked of each group. For example, these basic questions related to this cartoon could be used: (1) When Lucy says she wants all "ups," is she expressing a Christian attitude? (2) As a Christian what would you have Charlie say to her next? (3) Do you ever feel this way? (4) How can Jesus' good news to mankind be proclaimed to Lucy in this predicament?

Perhaps you have seen the many Peanuts cartoons in which Charlie's kite is caught and broken in the tree. What is the Christian answer for him? What situations in our lives are represented by Charlie's kite in the tree? The persons in one group might find that their "kite in the tree" is failing to keep their tempers again and again, constant frustration over trying to keep up with the housework, or meeting the weekly sales quota at the office. Class members might be asked to list several general "kites in the tree" which apply to their personal situations. Christian approaches to these problems could then be considered.

Different cartoons showing husband-wife relationships could be given to class members or to small groups within the class. Several questions to be discussed could be written on a chalkboard, such as these: (1) Are these people showing Christian love toward each other? (2) Is real acceptance shown? (3) Is the worth of the individual exhibited? (4) If not, how could the situation or dialogue be changed to show a Christian style of life? (5) What would the gospel say to these people?

With an unusual cartoon the caption might be clipped off before it is distributed and each person asked to write his own caption. These might be shared with the rest of the group. After some discussion these could be compared with the original caption.

Because cartoons appeal to a wide variety of people with varied backgrounds and perspectives, they offer a rich possibility of initiating stimulating, open conversation and discussion on a wide range of subjects.

Records and Pictures

Whether we preach the Word, sing it, make it visual, draw and color it, or express it through a multitude of other media, Christian faith has to be experienced to be personally real.

Why can't we use the recorded word, record or sound sheet, to serve as the confrontation of this "call and response" experience?

What if we turned our imagination loose on the use of records? One person who did, developed a presentation entitled "Theology of Sound." A young adult campus group was exposed to a variety of generalizations, stereotyped statements, and prejudicial remarks. After each negative thought, a portion of "message music" was played to provide the participant with "the other side." In that instance, it was difficult to hear some of the great Russian music and believe that "all Russians are Communists."

Or can we use the recorded message through song to show our people another side of the Negro, or any other object of concern? We need not suppose that this approach can be used only on the "hot issues." The record may be a very legitimate form of challenge to twentieth-century man.

What if we decided to use the record as a discussion launcher for our family night? We adults may have to take the initiative to suggest hearing something worthwhile, then listen for insights and reactions. Picture a family gathered to respond to the late Carl Michalson's recorded message on "The Hidden God" or, on the other side, "Anxiety." Speaking of home meetings, why shouldn't circles, apartment sets, or even coffee and conversation groups zero in on ideas or truths that might come from modern folk songs or other recorded or taped messages?

Perhaps we are conditioned by the state of mind that

leans toward having someone tell us the message—someone to make the message legitimate for us. However, we *must* have the interpersonal feeling if the Word is to be experienced.

In a day when we are getting away from our compartmentalized use of "religious" material, we need to look for the divine dimension in all of life. If the record can speak meaningfully to society at so many other points, can we afford not to see it as a legitimate tool for confrontation in our Christian teaching? Perhaps the challenge is to free ourselves to use *all* that is available—popular or not—to push us toward divine understanding.

Why should we not expose all Christians to this form of presentation? If adults, commission members, parents, or others, want to know what their young adult friends are thinking about the church, there is probably no better exposure than the record *Memo to a Parson*.[1] Again, the challenge is to turn ourselves loose to imaginative confrontation. The record provides a multitude of possibilities.

What if we decided to use the record only from some filmstrip packet? Has your group ever tried the combination of *hearing* and *expressing* as a means to the experiencing of faith? Suppose you were to expose your group to the recorded message and then ask them to create their own reactions on a mural, or even on individual "slides"? The resulting expression might be interesting, therapeutic, and even redemptive.

[1] *Memo to a Parson*. 17 minutes. Audiovisual Center, P.O. Box 871, Nashville, Tennessee 37202.

Three Examples

Now let's imagine ourselves as observers of three classes already in session.

Class No. 1 is using a presentation device combining records and pictures. The class is viewing a filmstrip with a recorded script. The projectionist is carefully following the script which indicates when each picture frame is to be changed.

The class leader has advised the group to listen for certain ideas relevant to the lesson. In this instance the filmstrip has two natural divisions: (1) the history of Brazilian missions and (2) the present work and cooperative efforts of these missions. After each section the leader has planned to stop the film and record to hear reports from the "listening groups" and to return to frames and recorded commentary that persons want repeated.

Class No. 2 is beginning a study of "The Inner City: A Seedbed for Delinquency." A member of the congregation who is a parole officer for the juvenile court has been asked to lead these sessions. He has gathered pictures of life in the inner city, including photographs of street children, gangs of loitering youth, and the almost unexpressive faces of adults caught in poverty's web.

As class members arrive, the juvenile officer invites them to study these pictures from three perspectives: (1) what they actually see regarding behavior, facial expression, and so on; (2) what they feel inwardly as they look at the pictures; (3) what they assume to be some of the problems related to the cultural islands and ghettos of the inner city.

After individual reflection on the pictures, the class

members are asked to form small groups and to discuss their observations and then to summarize their comments and reflections. Each group then reports its observations to the class, and the leader may relate facts gained from years of experience with juveniles in the inner city. Together, class and leader can uncover some areas of deep concern.

Class No. 3 is studying the attitudes of contemporary dramatists toward the meaning of life as conveyed in Archibald MacLeish's play, *J.B.* This morning they are listening to a recording of another play, *No Exit,* by Jean-Paul Sartre. After one sequence the leader stops the record and the people share what they have heard. They endeavor to compare Sartre's mood with that of MacLeish, and then they speculate as to what Sartre will have happen to his characters during the rest of the play. At the end, a comparison may be made between what happened in the play and what was anticipated and the reasons behind these differences in interpretation of meanings.

This class became interested in plays after reading *Contemporary Theatre and the Christian Faith,* by Kay Baxter.[2] They hesitated, however, simply to read and discuss the plays. Therefore, this class used records and other available resources to analyze plays, many of which seriously challenge the Christian viewpoint on matters of faith and morals. Members found themselves moved to analyze their own religious beliefs. One member reported, "I never have learned so much about my faith as when faced with the philosophy of an unbeliever."

* (Nashville: Abingdon Press, 1967.)

Objects

Do a little brainstorming. What are some of the three-dimensional objects readily available that can be used to enrich learning in your group?

Are there souvenirs and relics, "bits of reality" from other times and places you are studying? Do you have objects that represent and bring to mind biblical times, areas of missionary service, historical periods, other cultures, social situations, or segments of experience?

Can you make things to illustrate, symbolize, or focus attention on the concepts and issues in your study? Do not overlook such materials as pipe cleaners, plasticene, clay, papier-mâché, cardboard, or cloth.

What about objects that can be constructed during the learning process? Some interesting visual aids can be made out of blocks, clay, papier-mâché, and other odds and ends of materials. Often such constructions can be used by a group in making a report or in describing a particular process.

Your group has probably used some of these objects. You may have used them to create atmosphere for study, to focus attention, or to stimulate thinking. Perhaps you have used them to clarify, dramatize, or represent an abstract idea so that it could be handled and presented more easily. You may have found interesting objects from other times and cultures that helped students identify with the people involved.

Objects can be prepared by the leader, brought in by group members, or constructed in the study sessions. You can use them as exhibits or demonstrations to be looked at, as items to be handled and examined, or as materials to be manipulated, rearranged, and adjusted.

One group, examining the ways in which a local church might plan its programs, made a three-dimensional model of the administrative spiral. Another group that was discussing worship in the family constructed several home worship centers using the appropriate symbols. A third group studying John Wesley and the early Methodists found some old hymnbooks and class meeting tickets. They used all these objects in a display.

An adults' seminar interested in the generation gap made a collection of interesting objects from the "youth culture." They displayed earrings for pierced ears, a transistor radio with a lapel button pinned to it reading "Help! The paranoids are after me"; some magazines (*Accent on Youth, Mad, In, Teen, Cracked*); a record player and records (*The Ballad of Bonnie and Clyde, Honey,* Simon and Garfunkel's *Scarborough Fair, Forever Came Today* by the Supremes, and others); psychedelic posters; and many other typical objects.

The adults listened to the music, looked at the magazines, examined the other objects, and then shared their impressions. Here are some of their comments: "There are a number of paradoxes in this stuff." "I get a feeling of revolt, of reaction against." "The adult world portrayed in some of this is an upside down world." "My first impression is confusion, but I don't think it is all in me. Lots of this seems to be an expression of pressure and confusion." "Instant communication—the transistor, for example." "Yes, but I also hear some screaming as if they felt the adult world wasn't listening."

All this and more was triggered by these few objects.

Their thinking had been stimulated. Like magnets, the objects pulled together a number of ideas and feelings and stimulated their expression of them. The discussion did not stop with that, but went on to an evaluation of impressions.

Edgar Dale, in his definitive book on *Audio-Visual Methods in Teaching*,[1] discussed three-dimensional models under the heading "Contrived Experiences." He placed them in his famous "Cone of Experience" in the band next to "Direct Purposeful Experiences." This emphasizes their value as teaching tools. He described such objects as mock-ups, miniature working models, terrain models, globes, and specimens. These would be more complex and sophisticated objects than were suggested earlier, but they are not out of reach for use in the church's adult study.

In the last century local churches were encouraged to create large relief maps of Palestine on the church grounds so learners could imagine traveling around the Holy Land as they walked about the relief maps. The use of "stations of the cross" in Catholic devotions is another example of the use of objects to simulate an experience, such as that of going on a pilgrimage and living through the meanings that come from such an activity when the real experience is beyond reach. You can find similar ways to use objects in your church.

Exhibits

"A picture is worth a thousand words," according to an old adage. Unfortunately in many teaching/learning set-

[1] (New York: Holt, Rinehart and Winston, 1946), pp. 38-39.

tings the mouth and ears are used almost exclusively, with little opportunity for learning through other channels of communication.

In this article the word *exhibit* is used to mean any visual aid that might stimulate and encourage involvement of the adult in the learning situation. Old magazines, a supply of newsprint papers, some magic markers, scissors, and paste can provide material for meaningful visual exhibits.

Collage

In a series on the church, for example, groups might be able to make a collage to answer such questions as these:

What is the task of the church in the late twentieth century?

How is the church viewed by those within its membership? By those outside?

In making a collage, the members would go through the magazines looking for relevant pictures that might be used to cover a piece of newsprint or poster cardboard. Within the usual time allocated for classes—forty-five minutes to one hour—group members should be able to complete a collage twelve by twenty-four inches in size and explain it to the rest of the group. Not only pictures but a few pertinent words may be used on the collage.

A very helpful procedure for increasing the group's ability to work together is to agree that there must be group consensus before a picture is mounted. Members may wish to hang the collage in their study area until the completion of the unit, and references may be made to it as the study proceeds.

Life Needs

Another kind of exhibit might be a series of pictures that indicate some life needs of persons. These pictures should have captions, such as the following: "Do you know what it is like to be hungry?" "To be unwanted is to feel like this."

The pictures may start a group tackling a specific personal or community problem or need.

When a group is trying to develop greater sensitivity to the inner needs of persons, pictures or brief poems or short cuttings from a play may be displayed or distributed as discussion starters. Group members may discuss what they think is going on inside the persons presented in the pictures or the prose material. What are they saying? How are they feeling?

Sometimes it is easier for group members to express through a nonverbal medium the way they are feeling and sensing situations than through word forms. Using crayons and newsprint, persons may illustrate how they see the world, how they see communication within the group at that moment, or the way they are feeling.

At another time the group may be asked to do an exhibit that will deal with such questions as these: How do you see the world today? What does our community look like? How do youth feel about their world? How do youth see adults?

Bible and Newspaper

A very interesting way of making some biblical material come alive is to ask each group to work with the passage that is pertinent in the current study and then through whatever medium the members wish—a drawing, a role play, music, creative writing, or paraphrase—transform the passage from its biblical word pattern into an expression of their own.

The daily newspaper might very well be used as an exhibit. The articles, the advertisements, the comic strips hold great possibilities for getting the members involved in a search for meaning. Magazine covers may provide the starter that is needed.

Shock and Reaction

A rearrangement of the meeting room that may be a bit shocking to some of the members might be one kind of exhibit. For example, the usually orderly room may have paper on the floor, dust cloths on the chairs, and the chairs arranged in a disorganized fashion. This might start the group members on a consideration of their responsibilities as churchmen and members of the community.

As the members arrive, do they complain? Put the fault on the custodian? Sit down and leave things pretty much as they are? Or do they begin to do something about the conditions? Later they can discuss how they felt when they came in, what they did about it, and why. (A tape recorder could be used to get some of the impromptu comments.)

The more that group members can see the way in which the use of exhibits of various kinds can enhance the learning experience, the more initiative they will take for bringing these aids to the teaching setting, and the more they will learn as a group.

Factual Data

Without getting involved in philosophical discussions of the nature of fact, truth, or reality, let us define a fact as (1) a thing that has been experienced by the senses, (2) an event observed to have happened, and (3) information derived by calculation or experimentation. This book you are reading is a fact. That I wrote these words is a fact. That there were 840 words in this chapter before it was edited is a fact.

The use of factual data is emphasized in the physical and social sciences, in legal investigations, and in logical thinking. Facts are also important in many areas of study explored by church groups. Sometimes in religious discussions we run into difficulty because we confuse facts with opinions or depend on opinions at points where only facts are needed. Most of us who teach in the church have not developed the skills and procedures for the most effective use of factual data in our teaching and learning situations. The following observations might be helpful.

Bare facts are of little use until they are seen in relationship to other facts—to what one already knows, or to other kinds of knowledge. A study group might begin by collecting raw data, but the achievement of meanings will likely depend on discovering patterns in the data and relationships between these data and other facts. We need ways of organizing and reporting factual material so it can be studied and interpreted. This means learning how to make and use charts, diagrams, graphs, maps, and similar devices.

Time charts can be used when historical data are important to the study. The information the group has about a historical figure can be put on a time line. Other historical data—names, events, movements, artistic and literary creations—can be added. This can help us see the person in his historical context. We can better understand and more fully appreciate a person's life when we see its relation to what happened just before he lived, during his lifetime, and shortly after he died.

The time chart can be extended beyond the lifetime of a single person and can help us discover the parallelism between the lives of several persons who lived in different historical periods.

A time chart can be very helpful in showing the relation of different events and periods in biblical history.

Flow charts can be used when an organization or process is being studied. The data about how a local United Methodist church is organized and functions can be reduced to rectangles, lines, arrows, and circles and charted to show where different responsibilities and authorities reside and how they are related. Charts can be used to show the normal flow of the process by which a problem is located and analyzed, goals are set, a solution is proposed and evaluated, a decision to act is made, responsibility for acting is assigned, and the results are reviewed.

Charts are most useful if they are easy to read, are kept simple, and are not crowded. Color can be used to provide easier reading and interpretation.

Graphs are used when the data appear as numbers. Bar graphs help visualize relationships between numbers by using bar-shaped rectangles, representing the relative size of a given number. Church school attendance over a six-month period can be reported with a bar representing the number present on a given Sunday. These bars, side by side, show quickly the trends in attendance.

Graphs are more interesting when a row of outline figures (isotypes) are used in place of a solid bar. You can easily make an attendance chart similar to the production graph given on this page. On an attendance graph, for example, a human figure can represent a given number of persons, for instance, 10. Then 10 figures would represent 100 in attendance. If the group wants to compare the attendance trends for children, youth, and adults, different isotypes can be used for children, youth, and adults.

Year	Product A	Product B
1900	人人人人人	人人人人人人人人人
1920	人人人人人	人人人人人
1940	人人人人人	人人
1960	人人人	人人
1967	人	人

These are only samples of the ways factual materials can be presented. A little browsing through an encyclopedia, or a similar reference work, will suggest a number of additional devices and variations.

Newspapers and Magazines

Robert Short, in his interesting book, *The Gospel According to Peanuts,* says, " 'How shall we sing the LORD's song in a foreign land?' (Ps. 137:4) is a question the Church, always finding itself *in* but not *of* the world, urgently needs to reconsider today. For it not only needs to reconsider how it can best make meaningful contact with the particular men of our particular time . . . but the Church also needs to re-examine its strategy of communication to men of *all* times. . . ." [1]

Newspapers and magazines tend to focus on the hard issues and problems men face in their corporate and community life. The church can learn from these secular media much that concerns man and thus the needs to which the gospel must be addressed.

Mass communication media, represented in this article by newspapers and magazines, are an important influence in shaping and interpreting corporate and personal values in our society.

Since Christianity also deals with personal and social value systems and goals, groups engaged in serious study of Christian faith will find these media useful in confronting major issues and ideas.

If the comic strip "Peanuts," written by Charles Schulz, can convey deep theological ideas, as many people feel it does, it would seem to follow that other comic strips, editorials, and articles may be conveying equally important ideas. These media can be useful aids in adult study groups. If it is true that "a picture is worth a thousand words," it would seem that magazines and newspapers could be an excellent source for worthwhile pictures for use in adult study groups.

[1] Robert L. Short, *The Gospel According to Peanuts,* p. 7.

How may we use newspapers and magazines to good advantage in adult study? Here are some ideas:

1. *Post headlines, pictures, and articles* on bulletin boards or around the room to dramatize some concern for the Christian community. These should be in keeping with the study theme. Posting them in a prominent place in the room will provide maximum effect.

2. *Watch for series of articles that deal with relevant themes.* Series of articles are very common in daily newspapers and in major national magazines. These articles can bring a great deal of information to bear upon a given subject. Generally the writers of such a series of informative or interpretative articles must do a great deal of research. The articles will no doubt reflect a point of view, but this need not hinder their usefulness in your group. You can learn to cut through political and religious biases and get to the important data to be found in such articles.

3. *Editorials may be useful.* Editorial writers in magazines and newspapers generally seek to deal with broad community and world issues. Some editorial writers are very perceptive and portray good judgment in the analysis of problems and solutions. Others are highly opinionated and do not reflect broad vision. The point of view of the editorial need not negate its value, however. If group members recognize the point of view, evaluate the validity of it, and work through to their own conclusions, the poor editorial can be as useful as the good one.

4. *Columnists* sometimes have an inside track on what is really going on. Therefore, you need to be aware of the kinds of issues dealt with in the variety of columns carried in the typical daily newspaper and major magazines.

5. *Theological analysis* of newspaper articles and news

stories can be a learning experience. What is the theological rationale implicit in the article? Is there a doctrine of man that shows through? Theological points of view are often reflected in the way life issues are handled in the community. It could be a vital learning experience for a group to do a kind of theological analysis of some articles or news.

You will need to plan ahead if you are to make the best use of such resources. You might appoint a committee to glean articles and pictures that could be used during the study. This committee needs to have clearly in mind the type of things to look for and how to make use of them in the study sessions.

We are coming more and more to an understanding of man's wholeness. He is a "man in culture" and thus must be understood and dealt with in that context. If the message of the gospel is to be communicated to secular man, we must be willing to use all kinds of media.

Labor Unions

The American trade union movement has played a significant part in adult education. Through the years many labor organizations have employed professionally trained educators on the national and regional levels to develop educational programs and resources. They have specialized in teaching techniques and study resources that reach the man in the street. In their printed and projected materials they have paid attention to vocabulary, figures of speech, and illustrations that can be understood and responded to by persons our church efforts have sometimes bypassed. Some of the most worthwhile material on responsible citizenship in a democracy has come from this source.

These educational directors and coordinators are valuable persons to know. They can make available printed leaflets and booklets on some social and civil problems and issues. They are also a source for films and filmstrip. Each director has a trained staff of educators who are knowledgeable in many fields of interest to church study groups. All of them are skilled in adult education procedures, and many are willing to serve as resource persons on these matters.

Making Contact

How do you make contact with these educational resources? In each state capital and in most cities, there is an AFL-CIO Labor Council. This is a coordinating council for the several labor unions in the region. If you locate the address of one of these councils, you can easily find the educational coordinator. One address might be listed in your telephone book under Central Labor Council.

Inquiries can be made to the national headquarters about printed and projected resources and about the location of nearby labor councils. Direct your inquiries to AFL-CIO, 815 Sixteenth Street, Northwest, Washington, D.C. 20006.

Another place to request information or resources is the international headquarters of the Communications Workers of America. This is one of the few unions whose district educational coordinators cover the whole of the United States. From their headquarters you can find the name of the coordinator in your area. Address your letter to Communications Workers of America, 1925 K Street, Northwest, Washington, D.C. 20006.

When a study group uses resources from labor unions, they know the source and can take into account any bias they find. This is the same attitude we take toward resource material from business or any other organization that has a cause to promote or a point of view to propagate, and even with resource materials from the church. A particularly subjective bias might be counterbalanced by studying the other side's materials and viewpoints.

A desirable stance for a church study group is one of continual study and learning. An adult study group is a seeking group. Such a group begins with questions and not answers, and it assumes that the most valid answers will not be found in any one place, but will be derived from examining a variety of data and opinions.

A group of students in the District of Columbia met with a labor union spokesman to hear his comments on safety equipment on automobiles and the citizen's responsibility for highway safety. The student group was divided into three listening teams. The first was asked to listen for the speaker's basic assumptions. The second team listened for ideas he expressed that seemed to square with Christian ethics. And the third listened for ideas that seemed to be at variance with Christian ethics. The question period that followed the speech was not used up with insignificant questions. Instead, both the speaker and the students felt they got at the real issues involved.

Libraries

What is a library? A place posted with "Silence, please" signs where you can find dusty books in dingy stacks? Not anymore!

Libraries are concerned not only with books but with many other materials. They have files of pictures, films, filmstrips, recordings, color slides, projection equipment, maps, art objects, exhibits, pamphlet files, catalogs, and reference books of all kinds. Some have works of art for lending. In your library you may find files of "fugitive" materials—pamphlets, clippings, mimeographed and type-written items. There may be a file on the subject you are researching.

Many libraries have resource persons available to local groups. All have staff members who will aid you on any research problem you might have. Perhaps your local library is the most valuable resource for study helps in your community.

For example, if your group is studying famous persons, your library can be of help in several ways. You may find pictures of the times and persons you are studying. If they were authors, you may find their books. If an important work of someone you are studying is not in the local library, the librarian may be able to borrow it for you from another library through the interlibrary loan system.

Biographical information about persons of historical importance can be found in one or another of the reference works in your library's collection. Your library may have a set of *Butler's Lives of the Saints,* which lists the most familiar canonized saints of English-speaking Catholics. If the person you are studying is an American or an important figure in American history, you may refer to the twenty-volume *Dictionary of American Biography, Appleton's Cyclopaedia of American Biography, Who Was Who in America,* or some other biographical dictionary.

The chances are good that you can get information about a person you are studying from a number of biographical dictionaries and encyclopedias in your local library. Most librarians consider it a compliment when an interested person asks them to help find such information.

A group in Indiana was studying problems of the inner city. The chairman of the committee responsible for making study plans visited the city library and asked the circulation librarian where he could find books on the subject. He was surprised and pleased when she reached over to a rack and lifted from it a mimeographed bibliography. It contained a list of the books and periodical articles on the subject that were available in that library. Each had two- or three-sentence comments describing the content.

The librarian checked several she thought would be of most interest to his group. She identified two books that could be purchased in paperback editions at a nearby newsstand. Before he left, the chairman had arranged to borrow a collection of the books to put on display in their meeting room, and he got permission to make duplicate copies of the annotated bibliography.

When a library does not have a bibliography already prepared on a given subject, its staff is ready and willing to get together a display of books on the topic of your choice and, in many cases, to prepare and even duplicate in quantity an annotated bibliography.

Large libraries usually have a seasonal bulletin that announces the new books recently purchased. This listing contains a number of up-to-date books arranged by fields of interest. Other sources include the library's card file and other indexes.

Some library research requires more than simply locating books on the subject. For example, one should investigate two facts about books before giving a recommendation about them: Are they in print? Does the library have two or three copies of the book? The library staff is ready to help here, too. They will lead you to the research tools that can help unlock doors to the vast amount of information buried in their books and periodicals.

They will help you find, and show you how to use, such reference works as indexes to periodical material, various specialized dictionaries and encyclopedias, yearbooks, subject indexes, commentaries, concordances, and various standard collections. Staff members may do some of the research for you as part of their regular service.

In this article we have been speaking of the local community library. The same kinds of things can be said about other libraries that are available to you. Don't overlook the county library, your own church library and libraries in neighboring churches, public school libraries, libraries of nearby colleges and other educational institutions. In some communities organizations related to a profession or a business have libraries open to the public or material available on special request.

Well-informed Persons

"We killed our program by using resource persons." This comment was made in a discussion on adult education at Buck Hill Falls, Pennsylvania. This group member went on to say, "The only planning we did was to line up a series of speakers, and then we attended as spectators to see what kinds of speakers they were."

All agreed that this approach was a misuse of well-informed, or resource, persons. The Buck Hill Falls group went on to identify principles and procedures for effective use of resource persons. Here are some of their suggestions:

A study group should have a significant reason for inviting a resource person, a reason that is consistent with their study goals.

In some cases, an outsider might be brought in to help initiate a study. He might help identify the chief issues, suggest hypotheses to be tested, propose promising lines of investigation, and point to sources of information.

In another case a resource person might be brought in to supply needed information. When a study group needs data or opinions not found in the group or in printed resources at hand, a person knowledgeable in the field under consideration can help move the study forward. On another occasion this knowledgeable person might help the group review the results of its study and help them evaluate their findings.

An outside resource person can be useful in almost every stage of a group study program. It is important, however, to know what function he is to have and to be sure the group needs an outsider to perform this function.

The discussion group at Buck Hill Falls added other reasons a resource person might be used. He might provide face-to-face contact with a person representing a cause, a segment of society, or a culture in which the group is interested. He might stimulate the group members to work harder at their task by helping them clarify their goals and by reinforcing their purposes. He might demonstrate a study approach and help them develop skills in group study.

Regardless of the reason for using a resource person, the Buck Hill Falls group felt there were several steps that needed to be taken if the group were to profit from the experience. (1) The group needed to be prepared. (2) The resource person needed to be oriented to the group's study task. (3) Provision had to be made to keep the structure of the session in the hands of the group. (4) Follow-up had to be part of the plan.

Preparing the group. Before a resource leader comes, the group should know who he is and what he has to offer that fits their need. The reason he is being invited should be clear to all members. It might be helpful to have the group list what they want to find out from him. What questions do they want help on? What information do they need that he might have? They might also identify information they do not need from him and topics on which he might spend time if he is alerted. If the group has not been spending time studying in the area of his expertness, they may need considerable information from his area of study and experience.

Preparing the resource person. The visitor should be informed about what is wanted from him. He needs information about what the group has been studying, what it already knows, and why it needs his help. What is the area of concern to which they want him to address himself? What questions do they have? What problems? What information do they want? He needs to know, also, how the group operates. What is the format of the session?

147

What role is he expected to play? What role will the presiding person play? What can he expect by way of participation on the part of the group members?

Management of the session. A group member should direct the session and not turn it over to the visitor. This is not to suggest a mistrust of the visitor, rather it is a courtesy to him. The director of the session may introduce the guest speaker, but his responsibility does not end there. He might ask a few additional questions, if the group's response is disappointing, or channel the group's questions to the visitor. The visitor is meeting a specific need and will not have all responsibility for the group.

Follow-up. Evaluation can come either before or after the resource person leaves, in this class session or the next. The group should consciously relate the visitor's ideas to their plan of study. One good way to accomplish this would be through a comparison of their notes with the curriculum lesson materials. An evaluation should be as specific as possible and should concentrate on the points made by the resource person.

The group might try answering such questions as "What does this mean to us?" "Where do we go from here?" "Would we benefit by inviting our visitor back?"

Community Service Agencies

Probably many community service agencies, both governmental and voluntary, are located near your church. The number of such agencies increases as community life becomes more complex. Adults interested in the church and its mission should become increasingly aware of these agencies, learn about their activities, and find ways of cooperating with them when cooperation is appropriate. The purposes of many of them are related to purposes of the church. They can serve as valuable resources for enriching adult education activities.

Here are some ways adult study groups have related their studies to the resources of community service agencies:

1. A class committee visited the chief of police to inquire about safety on the streets and what citizens could do to help. They reported this information to the class, and a significant discussion followed.

2. A parent study group visited a Saturday night teen-age open house at the YMCA. They looked in on the swimming, watched the dancing and the floor show in the gym, and played pool and chess with some of the young people. Wandering from room to room they saw the variety of activities and observed what their community teen-agers do when they are offered choices. In their next meeting they shared ideas about teen-agers and about this type of community service. As a result, several of the class volunteered to help at the local YMCA.

3. A study of the alcohol problem and a discussion of social drinking became more personal by the use of two resource persons from Alcoholics Anonymous.

4. A class committee reported on safety practices for drivers and distributed literature they received from the local American Automobile Association.

5. A sex education film was borrowed by one group from the county Planned Parenthood Association. This

organization can provide pamphlets, charts, and many other materials.

6. The Goodwill Industries of one town provided a service outlet for one class. Class members worked in its "economy store," related to the people who shopped there, and found their world of experience and understanding expanding. This involvement influenced their choice of class study units and the direction of their discussions.

7. Persons, audiovisuals, printed materials, firsthand experiences, and many other study resources are available from community service agencies. These organizations are usually open to requests for information about their program and activities.

Finding Agencies

You know where some of these agencies are located in your city or town or county. How do you find others? One simple way is to look in the yellow pages of your telephone directory. Voluntary service agencies are usually listed under "Social Service Organizations," "Associations," and "Homes and Institutions." Government agencies may be found under "City Government," "County Government," and "National Government."

If your yellow pages do not help, you might turn to the alphabetical telephone list and look for "American Association of . . . ," "Association of . . . ," "Catholic . . . ," "Council of . . . ," "County . . . ," "International . . . ," "Jewish . . . ," "League of . . . ," "Metropolitan . . . ," "National . . . ," "Society . . . ," "Women's . . .".

Another reference tool for locating service agencies that can be found in the library is the *Social Work Year Book*.

This volume contains a directory of agencies with their national and regional offices and information about their activities. The agencies are listed in alphabetical order and can be located easily. This Association publishes an *Encyclopedia of Social Work* that is very helpful.

Serious study by church adults often leads to group action. Some community service agencies should be regarded not only as resources but as potential partners in action. Using these agencies and their resources in study is one way to encourage follow-through. When the study group decides on action, significant contacts are already established.

This happened in an Ohio church when a group concerned about children with special educational needs invited an officer from the county mental hygiene society to speak to them. He told about a new organization of parents of retarded children who were trying to start a through-the-week program. The local librarian, a member of the church study group, thought the library board would be willing to provide space. Class members looked further and found that some board of education funds could be tapped. They voted to contact the parents' group and assist them in their efforts. A school for exceptional children was the result.

Take advantage of the local service agencies and their free resources.

National Organizations

Helpful resources are available from many of our national organizations and associations. On pages 141-42 we referred to two labor organizations. The 1971 *World Almanac* lists over 1,000 national organizations. Many of these have literature and films that can be secured free or with little cost. Some have state and local units with personnel willing to serve as resource persons in local church groups.

The following is a random sample of these organizations listed in categories that might suggest their relationship to adult study topics.

Cause-oriented Organizations

National Safety Council, 425 North Michigan Avenue, Chicago, Illinois 60611
Carnegie Endowment for International Peace, 345 East Forty-sixth Street, New York, New York 10017
American Civil Liberties Union, Inc., 156 Fifth Avenue, New York, New York 10010
League of Women Voters of the United States, 1026 Seventeenth Street, Washington, D.C. 20036
Southern Christian Leadership Conference (civil rights), 334 Auburn Avenue, Northeast, Atlanta, Georgia 30303
National Association for the Advancement of Colored People, 30 West Fortieth Street, New York, New York 10018

Organizations with a Religious Emphasis

American Bible Society, 450 Park Avenue, New York, New York 10023
American Jewish Congress, 15 East Eighty-fourth Street, New York, New York 10028
National Conference of Christians and Jews, Inc., 43 West

Fifty-seventh Street, New York, New York 10019
Religious Education Association, 545 West 111th Street,
New York, New York 10025

Organizations with a Recreational and Leisure-time Emphasis

American Association for Health, Physical Education, and
Recreation, 1201 Sixteenth Street, Northwest, Washington, D.C. 20036
National Audubon Society, 1130 Fifth Avenue, New York,
New York 10028
American Camping Association, Bradford Woods, Martinsville, Indiana 46151

Service Clubs and Fraternities

Lions International, 209 North Michigan Avenue, Chicago, Illinois 60601
United States Junior Chamber of Commerce (Jaycees),
Boulder Park, Box 7, Tulsa, Oklahoma 74102
General Federation of Women's Clubs, 1734 N Street,
Northwest, Washington, D.C. 20036

Organizations Concerned for the Handicapped

National Society for Crippled Children and Adults, Inc.,
2023 West Ogden Avenue, Chicago, Illinois 60612
National Association for Retarded Children, 386 Park
Avenue, South, New York, New York 10017
National Society for the Prevention of Blindness, 16 East
Fortieth Street, New York, New York 10016

Organizations Interested in Promoting Health

National Association for Mental Health, Inc., 10 Columbus Circle, New York, New York 10019

American Cancer Society, Inc., 219 East Forty-second Street, New York, New York 10017

Professional and Vocational Organizations

American Nurses' Association, 10 Columbus Circle, New York, New York 10019

Farmers' Educational and Cooperative Union of America, 1575 Sherman Street, Denver, Colorado 80201

National Small Business Association, 801 Nineteenth Street, Northwest, Washington, D.C. 20036

Organizations with an Interest in Education

Adult Education Association of the United States of America, 743 North Wabash Avenue, Chicago, Illinois 60611

National Education Association, 1201 Sixteenth Street, Northwest, Washington, D.C. 20036

National Congress of Parents and Teachers, 700 North Rush Street, Chicago, Illinois 60611

American Association of University Women, 2401 Virginia Avenue, Northwest, Washington, D.C. 20037

Many of these organizations, and others, publish periodicals, some of which are in your local library.

Biographical Notes

Dr. Howard H. Bright, Jr., is an associate professor and chairman of the department of sociology and anthropology at West Virginia Wesleyan College, Buckhannon, West Virginia.

The Rev. Robert P. Crosby is a training and organizational consultant in Spokane, Washington.

The Rev. Fred H. Kight is program minister at Belle Meade United Methodist Church, Nashville, Tennessee.

The Rev. Patricia Sailors Kirton, a minister of education in the Rocky Mountain Conference (United Methodist), is a part-time chaplain (pediatric) at Denver General Hospital.

Taylor and June McConnell live in Evanston, Illinois. Mrs. McConnell is a free-lance writer and lab leader, and Dr. McConnell is a professor at Garrett Theological Seminary.

The Rev. Charles E. Mowry is president of Midcontinent Consultants and MIDCO Educational Associates in Denver, Colorado.

Dr. Robert Richard Powell is professor of Christian education at Wesley Theological Seminary in Washington, D.C.

The Rev. Roy H. Ryan is director of Middle Adult Ministries for the United Methodist Board of Education in Nashville.

The Rev. Lon A. Speer is editor of *Our Living Bible* in the Department of Adult Publications of The United Methodist Church, Nashville.

Georgia M. Sprinkle is assistant professor of education at Mt. Union College, Alliance, Ohio.

Bibliography

Adult Education Association of the U.S.A. *How to Teach Adults* (Leadership Pamphlet #5). Chicago, 1956.

———. *How to Lead Discussions* (Leadership Pamphlet #1). Chicago, 1955.

Barnlund, Dean C., and Haiman, Franklyn S. *The Dynamics of Discussion*. Boston: Houghton Mifflin, 1960.

Bergevin, Paul; Morris, Dwight; and Smith, Robert M. *Adult Education Procedures*. New York: The Seabury Press, 1963.

Blake, Robert R., and Mouton, Jane S. *Group Dynamics: Key to Decision Making*. Houston: Gulf Publishing Company, 1961.

Boehlke, Robert R. *Theories of Learning in Christian Education*. Philadelphia: Westminster Press, 1963.

Bruner, Jerome S. *The Process of Education*. Vintage Books; New York: Random House, 1960.

Casteel, John L., ed. *Creative Role of Interpersonal Groups in the Church Today*. New York: Association Press, 1968.

Dawson, Helaine S. *On the Outskirts of Hope*. New York: McGraw-Hill, 1968.

Dichter, Ernest. *Motivating Human Behavior*. New York: McGraw-Hill, 1971.

Du Bois, Rachel Davis, and Li, Mew-Soong. *The Art of Group Conversation*. New York: Association Press, 1963.

Flinders, Neil J. *Personal Communications*. Salt Lake City: Deseret Book Company, 1966.

Fritz, Dorothy Bertolet. *Ways of Teaching*. Philadelphia: Westminster Press, 1965.

Ghiselin, Brewster, ed. *The Creative Process*. Mentor Books; New York: New American Library, 1952.

Gowan, John Curtis; Demos, George D.; and Torrance, E. Paul, Compilers. *Creativity: Its Educational Implications.* New York: Wiley, 1967.

Harris, Thomas. *I'm OK—You're OK.* New York: Harper, 1969.

Howe, Reuel L. *Survival Plus.* New York: The Seabury Press, 1972.

Jones, Richard M. *Fantasy and Feeling in Education.* New York: New York University Press, 1968.

Jourard, Sidney M. *The Transparent Self.* New York: Van Nostrand, 1971.

Knowles, Malcolm S. *Informal Adult Education.* New York: Association Press, 1950.

Leslie, Robert C. *Sharing Groups in the Church.* Nashville: Abingdon Press, 1971.

McBurney, James H., and Hance, Kenneth G. *Discussion in Human Affairs.* New York: Harper, 1950.

Mager, Robert F. *Preparing Instructional Objectives.* Palo Alto, Calif.: Fearon Publishers, 1962.

Maltz, Maxwell. *Psycho-Cybernetics.* North Hollywood: Wilshire Book Company, 1970.

Middleman, Ruth R. *The Non-verbal Method in Working with Groups.* New York: Association Press, 1968.

Miel, Alice, ed. *Creativity in Teaching.* Belmont, Calif.: Wadsworth Publishing Company, 1961.

Minor, Harold D., ed. *Creative Procedures for Adult Groups.* Nashville: Abingdon Press, 1968.

Organ, Troy Wilson, and Garvin, Lucius. *The Art of Critical Thinking.* Boston: Houghton Mifflin, 1965.

Postman, Neil, and Weingartner, Charles. *Teaching as a Subversive Activity.* New York: Delacorte Press, 1969.

Raths, Louis E.; Harmin, Merrill; and Simon, Sidney B. *Values and Teaching.* Columbus: Charles E. Merrill, 1966.

Rich, John Martin. *Education and Human Values.* Reading, Mass.: Addison-Wesley, 1968.

Rogers, Carl R. *Carl Rogers on Encounter Groups.* New York: Harper, 1970.

————. *Freedom to Learn.* Columbus: Charles E. Merrill, 1969.

Schwartz, William, and Zalba, Serapio R. *Practice of Group Work.* New York: Columbia University Press, 1971.

Shinn, Roger L. *The Educational Mission of Our Church.* Philadelphia: United Church Press, 1962.

Silberman, Charles E. *Crisis in the Classroom.* Vintage Books; New York: Random House, 1970.

Slusser, Gerald H. *A Dynamic Approach to Church Education.* Geneva Press; Philadelphia: Westminster Press, 1968.

Stenzel, Anne K., and Feeney, Helen M. *Learning by the Case Method.* New York: The Seabury Press, 1970.

Swain, Dorothy G. *Teach Me to Teach.* Valley Forge, Pa.: Judson Press, 1964.

Torrance, E. Paul. *Education and the Creative Potential.* Minneapolis: The University of Minnesota Press, 1967.

Whitehead, Alfred North. *The Aims of Education.* New York: Macmillan, 1959.